Hebrews

T&T CLARK STUDY GUIDES TO THE NEW TESTAMENT

Series Editor

Tat-siong Benny Liew, College of the Holy Cross, USA

Other titles in the series include:

T&T Clark Study Guides to the Old Testament:

Hebrews

An Introduction and Study Guide

Patrick Gray and Amy Peeler

t&tclark

LONDON • NEW YORK • OXFORD • NEW DELHI • SYDNEY

T&T CLARK
Bloomsbury Publishing Plc
50 Bedford Square, London, WC1B 3DP, UK
1385 Broadway, New York, NY 10018, USA

BLOOMSBURY, T&T CLARK and the T&T Clark logo are trademarks of Bloomsbury
Publishing Plc

First published in Great Britain 2020

Cover design by clareturner.co.uk

A catalogue record for this book is available from the British Library.

A catalog record for this book is available from the Library of Congress.

ISBN: HB: 978-0-5676-9481-2
ISBN: PB: 978-0-5676-7475-3
ePDF: 978-0-5676-7476-0
ePUB: 978-0-5676-7477-7

Series: T&T Clark's Study Guides to the New Testament

Typeset by Deanta Global Publishing Services, Chennai, India

To find out more about our authors and books visit www.bloomsbury.com
and sign up for our newsletters.

Contents

Preface

This volume offers a concise introduction to one of the most daunting texts in the New Testament. The Letter (or Sermon?) to the Hebrews has inspired many readers with its encomium or tribute to faith, troubled others with its hard sayings on the impossibility of a second repentance, and perplexed still others with its exegetical assumptions and operations drawn from a cultural matrix that is largely alien to modern sensibilities. Long thought to be Paul, the anonymous author of Hebrews exhibits points of continuity with the apostle and other New Testament writers in the letter's (or sermon's) vision of life in the light of the crucified Messiah, but one also finds distinctive perspectives in such areas as Christology, eschatology, and atonement.

The introduction surveys the salient historical, social, and rhetorical factors to be considered in the interpretation of Hebrews. Chapter 1 provides a brief commentary on the text. Chapter 2 discusses recent scholarship on the teaching of Hebrews as it relates to the Holy Spirit. Chapter 3 examines the history of interpretation of Hebrews from antiquity to the present, with special attention to its theological, liturgical, and cultural legacy outside the precincts of the academy. Questions for further study are included to aid groups or individuals who wish to engage more deeply with one of the most original Christian writers of the first century.

References to God as "Father" (with accompanying male pronouns) appear in our discussion of Hebrews. We employ this language to follow the terminology employed by this ancient author whose letter refers to God as "Father" twice (1:5; 12:9). Feminist critiques of such language rightly name the incorrect assumption that it often imports, namely, that God is male. New Testament texts as well as Christian traditions have rejected this assumption; instead, many affirm that God is spirit. For this author of Hebrews, we argue that paternal language captures the personal nature of God and the intimate relationship this God has with Jesus and with those who are followers of Jesus, especially as they relate to the issues of education and inheritance closely related to the family in the author's sociocultural context. We wish for this language not to be a distraction but to point toward the text and to the realities this language communicated for the author and the community to whom the author was writing.

Introduction

Who wrote the Letter to the Hebrews? When was it written? What can be known about its intended audience? What prompted its composition, and what did the author hope to achieve? Is it, in fact, a letter, or does it belong to some other genre? These and other introductory questions will be discussed before proceeding to a more detailed treatment of the text in the following chapter.

Author

Listening to a symphony without knowing the name of the composer or gazing at a work of art without knowing who painted it can be a disorienting experience. In much the same way, reading a text without knowing who wrote it can likewise be discomfiting. If only for psychological reasons, then, the earnest efforts to identify the author of the Letter to the Hebrews from antiquity to the present come as little surprise. The list of candidates is perhaps longer for Hebrews than for any other book in the New Testament. Patristic interpreters put forth a number of names, with the apostle Paul receiving the most attention (see below). As soon as his name emerges, it is clear that other figures had already been associated with the letter (Eusebius, *Hist. eccl.* 3:38; 6:14, 25). Clement of Alexandria late in the second century claims that Luke was responsible for translating into Greek a Hebrew original produced by Paul. Origen similarly remarks that the thoughts might be those of Paul but the language is not, mentioning that Clement of Rome had been proposed as the author but concluding that "God knows" who actually wrote it. Tertullian (*Pud.* 20) quotes Hebrews and attributes it to Barnabas, who had also been credited with writing a second-century epistle that touches on some of the same themes as Hebrews.

These few names mentioned as possibilities by patristic writers are each discussed in relation to Paul, either on stylistic grounds or in connection with the passing reference to Timothy in Heb. 13:23. Yet Marcion does not include it among Paul's letters, and though it is commonly accepted in the Eastern church, doubts as to its Pauline authorship are widespread in the West from an early date. Its delayed inclusion in the canon was in no small measure a function of these lingering doubts. Athanasius lists Hebrews among Paul's letters in his Thirty-Ninth Festal Letter of 367, but as late as 397 the Synod of Carthage reflects uncertainty in speaking of "the thirteen epistles of the Apostle Paul" and only then adding one epistle "to the Hebrews, by the same."

Reformation-era critics shift their focus from style to content. Luther could not square the apparent prohibition of repentance for post-baptismal sin in Heb. 6:4-6 with Paul's emphasis on God's grace extended to sinners. Erasmus and Calvin likewise sense differences between the teachings of Paul and of Hebrews but do not share Luther's reservations about the latter's place in the canon. (Luther places Hebrews alongside James, Jude, and Revelation at the end of his 1522 edition of the German New Testament, indicating his theological qualms about its status.) On the Catholic side, the Council of Trent in 1546 includes Hebrews among the Pauline letters and affirms its status as Scripture. The King James Version of 1611 follows suit in attributing it to Paul in the title.

The view that Paul wrote Hebrews enjoys very little support among modern scholars. To be sure, Hebrews and Paul's writings share a number of concerns. Both authors envision Jesus as having a role in creation before obediently humbling himself and taking on human nature (Heb. 1:2-3; 2:14-17; cf. Rom. 8:3; 1 Cor. 8:6; 2 Cor. 4:4; Gal. 4:4; Phil. 2:6-8). They emphasize faith in the relationship between God and humanity and cite Abraham as an exemplar of how this relationship may unfold (Heb. 11:11-12, 17-19; Rom. 4:1-25). They refer to a number of the same biblical texts in making their arguments (e.g., Deut. 32:35 in Rom. 12:19 and Heb. 10:30; Psalm 8 in 1 Cor. 15:27 and Heb. 2:6-9; Hab. 2:4 in Rom. 1:17; Gal. 3:11; and Heb. 10:38). And it is worth noting that Hebrews never circulated independently of the Pauline corpus in the surviving manuscript tradition.

Notwithstanding these similarities, the differences are perhaps more pronounced. As ancient readers note, the language and style are not like those of Paul. Shared terminology is often used in different ways, as when Hebrews speaks of "righteousness" in ethical terms (1:9; 12:4) rather than in the forensic sense favored by Paul (e.g., Rom. 2:13; 4:1-25). Their vocabularies also differ in that Hebrews refers to Jesus by name far more frequently than Paul, who uses the titles Christ and Lord more often. The substance of their respective teachings also differs. The dominant image of Jesus as high priest has no parallel in Paul's letters. Both authors accentuate Jesus's death, but cross imagery occurs more regularly and more explicitly in Paul than in Hebrews. As for what follows the cross, Hebrews dwells on Jesus's exaltation to the right hand of God in heaven more so than on the resurrection per se. While the new covenant motif can be found in Paul—for instance, in 2 Cor. 3:6, where it is elaborated in connection with Exod. 34—it receives nowhere near the same emphasis as it does in Hebrews, where it is drawn from the oracle of Jer. 31:31-34. The critique of the old covenant in Hebrews, moreover, focuses chiefly on aspects of its sacrificial system rather than on the legal and ethical dimensions of Torah.

Three other considerations militate against Pauline authorship. Hebrews appears to situate itself within a slightly different historical context from what one would expect for Paul. In Heb. 2:3, the author says of the good news, "It was declared at first through the Lord, and it was attested to us by those who heard him." Paul's insistence that the source of his gospel is "through a revelation of Jesus Christ" and not "from a human source" makes it difficult to imagine coming from his lips such a confession of reliance on human intermediaries, apostolic or not (Gal. 1:11-12). Furthermore, the Jew-Gentile tensions that can be felt in nearly every one of Paul's letters are absent from Hebrews, as are the sophisticated theological attempts he makes to explain their relationship in God's providential plan. Last, and certainly not least, the most basic reason to come down against Pauline authorship is that the letter nowhere explicitly claims to be written by Paul. It has been argued that the postscript referring to Timothy in Heb. 13:23 is an implicit, if pseudepigraphical, assertion of Pauline authorship (Rothschild 2009: 67–81). The hypothesis is an intriguing one but at points seems to assume what it sets out to prove, namely, that an anonymous author coyly demurs from referring to himself as Paul so as to convince readers that he is in fact Paul. While the differences between Hebrews and Paul's letters may not amount to outright contradictions, they place the burden of proof on anyone positing Pauline authorship for a document that nowhere lays claim to it.

Luther's judgment on the theological value of Hebrews does not carry the day, but he launches a cottage industry of sorts among scholars when he reopens the case against Pauline authorship. The list of potential authors suggested in the following centuries is a veritable "Who's Who" of the early church. Luther himself speculated that it was Apollos, the Alexandrian Jew mentioned in Acts 18:24-28. His eloquence and deep knowledge of the Jewish Scriptures in the Septuagint version (LXX) certainly seems to fit the profile of the author. Taking this theory one step further are scholars who suggest that the author was Priscilla, who, along with her husband Aquila, instructed Apollos in the Christian faith (with the letter's abiding interest in the tabernacle rather than the temple sometimes explained by the couple's occupation as tentmakers!). Also from the cast of characters in Acts, similarities between Acts 7 and the critique of Israelite worship and the survey of Jewish history in Hebrews 9–11 have led others to wonder whether Stephen might be the author. Of course, since he is stoned to death immediately after giving this speech, he would have had little time for writing about those subjects in letters. Adjusting the theory to accommodate Stephen's untimely demise, advocates of this view surmise that one of his fellow Hellenists, such as Philip the deacon, or else Luke might be responsible for transmitting his teachings to the Hebrews. Other suggestions, such as Epaphras, Jude, and Mary the mother of Jesus, have even less evidence in their favor. At least the ancient suggestions of Luke and Clement permit some literary standard for comparison. Many of the modern theories are tantalizing but, as the various candidates have left no writings of their own, there is no basis for proving them. By the same token, neither is there any way to disprove them, which helps to explain why they refuse to die.

While the name of the author remains out of reach, it is nonetheless possible to make a number of observations about the person who wrote Hebrews—for example, that the person is probably a man, if the self-referential masculine participle used in Heb. 11:32 is any indication. (For this reason, although Ruth Hoppin [1969] and Cynthia Briggs Kittredge [1994] have argued for a female author, we believe that it is far more likely that the author is male and will thus refer to him as "he.") Not only is he steeped in the Jewish Scriptures in their Septuagint form, he also writes about them in perhaps the most polished Greek in the entire New Testament. By itself, his familiarity with the Law, the Prophets, and the Writings is not proof that he hails from a Jewish background, but his apparent familiarity with midrashic interpretive techniques makes it less likely that he is a Gentile believer in Jesus. He enjoys the respect of his readers as a teacher if not as an apostle who walked with the Lord. His impressive rhetorical skill, perhaps acquired through formal education in a Greek or Roman setting, no doubt contributes to his status in this respect. (It may also be that a self-deprecating sense of humor endears him to his audience, as when he says in Heb. 13:22, at the end of thirteen chapters of dense exposition, that he has written to them "briefly.") He is personally acquainted with his audience and has plans to visit them in the near future (13:19, 23). For these and any other details about the author, modern readers must rely on what he has revealed through the letter he has left behind.

Audience

To whom was the Letter to the Hebrews written? It seems like a trick question. Was it not written to "the Hebrews"? If only it were so straightforward. The audience is never addressed as such by the author, and the earliest surviving occurrence of the superscript *pros Ebraious* ("to the Hebrews") does not occur until it appears in a papyrus copy of the letter (P^{46}) dating to the late second or early third century. Insofar as "Hebrew" in the first century was a linguistic marker denoting a speaker of Hebrew or Aramaic as much as an ethnic or religious group (Acts 6:1; 22:2; Phil. 3:5), it seems somewhat inappropriate for the readers of a text written in Greek (Koester 2001: 171–72). Suspecting that the title amounts to no more than an educated guess on the part of early scribes—using archaizing nomenclature at that—many scholars believe the author is in fact writing to Gentiles. Whatever shortcomings he discerns in the former covenant described in the Old Testament, it would be jarring to hear the alternative—to progress in faith and thus a putative return to their former life in Judaism—described as "falling away from the living God" (3:12; cf. 1 Thess. 1:9). Parallels between the catechesis for Gentile proselytes in Second Temple Judaism and the fundamentals of the faith listed in Heb. 6:1-2 further hint at a non-Jewish audience (Braun 1984: 157–60).

However plausible, modern theories about a Gentile readership are likewise educated guesses, and a majority of scholars more or less agree with the traditional view that the original audience consisted of Christians who were "descendants of Abraham" (2:16). Few would be so specific as to assert that, for example, they had been priests in Jerusalem or converts from the Essene community at Qumran, but the argument assumes a degree of familiarity with Jewish tradition rarely matched in the New Testament. If the author is as rhetorically gifted as is generally believed, it would be obtuse for him to argue in a manner that his audience could not appreciate, and as the letter was saved and circulated, one may cautiously surmise that the original audience could digest its contents and deemed it worthy of preservation. The Jewish roots of Roman Christianity and the similarities between Hebrews and Hellenistic synagogue homilies also suggest but by no means prove that the audience had a background in Judaism.

Ultimately, it is impossible to separate questions about the audience from those about the author's objectives (see "Occasion and Purpose"). For example, the hypothesis that the audience is tempted to "return" to Judaism is incompatible with a Gentile readership, though a document like Galatians shows that one need not be Jewish in order to "turn" to some form of Jewish belief or practice. Moreover, based simply on the information found in the letter, it might be difficult to distinguish a Jewish audience from an audience of Gentile God-fearers who had been socialized and instructed in a Hellenistic synagogue. And what should one expect to find if the audience were "mixed"? One sees neither the hints of friction found in Romans nor the irenic tone of Ephesians with its reference to "the dividing wall" having been torn down (Eph. 3:14). It may be that, in the absence of any mention of ethnic harmony or hostility, Hebrews is less likely to be addressed to a mixed audience, and that a Jewish background fits the facts gleaned from the text more so than a Gentile background. At any rate, the author is not primarily concerned with where his readers are coming from, ethnically or even religiously speaking, but with where he hopes or fears they are headed.

The letter reveals more about the audience's social circumstances than about their religious or ethnic background, and this information proves to be more useful in putting the author's message in context. Although his observations and admonitions may be applicable to a general Christian readership, he is clearly addressing a specific community of indeterminate size with whom he hopes soon to be reunited (13:23). They may comprise one house church among several in a large city. Their conversion is not a recent event, as the author thinks they ought to have made more progress "by this time" (5:12). In connection with their newfound faith, they have endured some type of harassment. Their possessions have been plundered and some have been thrown in jail, though none have been put to death (10:32-34; 12:3-4; 13:3). Perhaps to avoid inconvenient associations that would lead to additional mistreatment, members have begun to absent themselves from communal gatherings (10:25). The author perceives a certain weakening of their faith in their response to these hardships (2:1-3; 3:12-14; 4:11; 10:35; 12:3, 12). Other specific questions and what they may or may not reveal about the audience—for example, did they venerate angels (1:5-14)? were they contemplating apostasy or had some of them already taken that step (6:4-6)? were there tensions between "leaders" and "laity" (13:7, 17)?—will be addressed in the commentary devoted to particular passages. While the author's message is not entirely contingent on the profile of the audience and exposition of the text is not the same as reconstructing the particular situation they were facing, tentative answers to many of these contextual questions aid in the letter's exegesis.

Provenance and destination

Hebrews lacks a formal salutation that places the audience on the map. The author also does not bother with a return address that reveals the location from which he is writing. The most telling clue comes near the end when he says that "those from Italy send greetings" (13:24). Does this point to an Italian provenance or destination? While it is conceivable that the author is writing from Italy to Christ-believers who are from Italy but are now residing elsewhere, it would seem more customary to say "we who are in Italy." Moreover, the syntax (*apo tēs Italias*) more strongly connotes a group that is sending greetings back to Italian friends from whom they have been separated. The author may be among Jewish Christians like Priscilla and Aquila who had been exiled from the capital by Claudius in 49 CE (Acts 18:2)—references to this decree by Roman writers such as Suetonius suggest that the authorities did not always distinguish between Christ-believing and non-messianist Jews—though the location of the home away from Rome of any such exiles could be almost anywhere. The circumstances of the audience matter more to the author than those where he happens to be when he puts pen to paper.

And where are his readers? Proponents of a destination in the environs of Jerusalem point to the letter's special interest in the sacrificial cult and the fact that it would be more likely to find a Jewish-Christian readership there. But again, the focus is on the tabernacle and not the temple, and, moreover, early Christian writers not infrequently expect readers in the Diaspora to have an interest in biblical matters connected to Palestine. In addition, unlike the audience of Hebrews, it appears that Christ-believers in Jerusalem had indeed suffered "to the point of shedding blood" (12:4; cf. Acts 7:58-60; 1 Thess. 2:14-16). Alexandria has also been put forward as a possibility on the grounds that the letter's affinities with the writings of Philo would be appreciated by that city's Hellenized Jewish population. But this might apply as well to Greek-speaking Jews or Jewish Christians in other large cities such as Antioch or Caesarea.

Rome or somewhere else on the Italian peninsula is the more likely destination to which Hebrews was sent. Readers in the capital would naturally welcome the greetings from the Italians relayed by the author. Members of the Christian community in Rome had also experienced social pressures at various times, though gaps in the historical record and the lack of details in the letter make it impossible to say with certainty that Rome is the setting for Hebrews. That the earliest external attestation comes in *1 Clement* constitutes stronger evidence. The quotations of Hebrews in this letter written in Rome shows that before the turn of the century it was being read in the Eternal City, as it was called by such writers as Tibullus, Ovid, and Virgil from the time of the late Republic. For Christians making their way in the *Urbs Aeterna*, the poignant reminder that they have "no lasting city, but look forward to a city which is to come" (13:14) might have held special meaning.

Date

That Hebrews was written sometime in the first century is widely acknowledged, as it is known by *1 Clement* and most scholars date the latter near the end of Domitian's reign in 96 CE. Is it possible to locate the author and audience with greater specificity? Scholars frequently refer to early Christian writings, vaguely, as "early" or "late," which is often shorthand for pre- or post-70 CE. On the early side, the only firm point before which Hebrews cannot have been written is the death of Jesus *c.* 30 CE. Allowing for even the most rudimentary theological reflection and community growth, along with the author's chiding of his readers for their lack of growth despite having been believers for some time (5:11-12), it seems unlikely that it was written prior to the mid-40s. Another indication relevant to an early dating is usually seen in Heb. 2:3, where the author mentions that the good news "was declared at first through the Lord, and it was attested to us by those who heard him." This is often taken as evidence that they belong to the "second generation" of believers, but in reality, it rules out nothing more than a claim to being an eyewitness to the earthly ministry of Jesus. Dependence on "those who heard him" hardly necessitates the passage of decades, as the same could easily have been said about the audiences for much of the earliest Christian preaching.

There is little in Hebrews that requires a late dating. It details no elaborate organization and prescribes no "church order" like one finds in the second century and is often labeled "early Catholicism." Offhand references to "leaders" (13:7, 17) are the only indication of "hierarchy" to be found. Polemic against heresy of the sort that becomes common with the emergence of Gnosticism is likewise missing. The allusion to persecution (10:32-34; 12:5; 13:3, 13) might reflect circumstances under either Nero in the 60s or Domitian in the 90s. As most harassment was local and sporadic rather than empire-wide and officially sanctioned, and with so few of the particulars spelled out, the description in Hebrews could fit almost any time or place. The fraught relationship between Jews and Gentiles which so consumes Paul is not in evidence, perhaps because it has yet to become a pressing issue or else is part of the fading past. Yet this, too, is inconclusive since the so-called parting of the ways between church and synagogue occurs at different times in different regions. Some see in the opening verses a view of Jesus as divine or quasi-divine—he is "the reflection of God's glory and the exact imprint of God's very being" (1:3)—that amounts to a "high" Christology which could only have developed after a decades-long period of theological gestation. But already in the 50s, Paul can describe Jesus as being "in the form of God" and worthy of homage as Lord (Phil. 2:6-11), apparently quoting a hymn which expresses an exalted conception of Jesus that had formed even earlier. More speculative still are theories relating the exaltation motif in Hebrews to the apotheosis of the Emperor Titus in Flavian propaganda and claiming that the author is familiar with a form of Mark's Gospel, either of which would point to a date of composition in the 70s or 80s (Aitken 2005: 131–48; Mitchell 2007: 10–11). Finally, the mention of Timothy's release from jail in Heb. 13:23, if he is Paul's young coworker of the same name, does little to narrow the range of possible dates, as it could fall at any point between the 50s to the end of the century.

How might the author have responded to the destruction of the temple in 70 CE? This is perhaps the most salient question in determining when Hebrews was written, even if answering it inevitably means relying on circumstantial evidence. It may be that the cessation of sacerdotal activities in Jerusalem is what prompted the author's meditations on the obsolescence of the Jewish priesthood. Just as the book of Ruth is sometimes thought to reflect contentious postexilic debates about intermarriage with non-Judeans in the time of Ezra but in the form of a story "once upon a time," set in the period prior to the Davidic monarchy, it may be that the author seeks to probe the theological dimensions of this first-century military catastrophe in the form of a complex analysis of the Levitical system described in the Pentateuch that had been instituted over a millennium earlier in the time of Moses. But the opposite seems more likely. That is, it is difficult to imagine an event more suited to punctuating an argument about the inherently provisional and temporary nature of the Jewish priesthood (Heb. 7:11-19) than the destruction of the temple. And yet the author says nothing of it. Surely the fall of the temple would have seemed like decisive confirmation of the exegetical case concerning Jewish sacrifice he painstakingly builds in Heb. 7:1–10:18, even if the discussion in those chapters deals with the tabernacle "tent of meeting" used in the wilderness wanderings of the Exodus generation and not the stone and mortar building in Jerusalem. The second-century *Epistle of Barnabas* connects the theological dots in a similar fashion, albeit more harshly than Hebrews in describing "how the wretched men erred by putting their hope on the building" which "was destroyed by the enemy" (16:1, 4). Hebrews states that the "first covenant" and its priesthood "is growing old and will soon disappear" (8:13); had he known of the events that transpired in 70 CE, could he have resisted phrasing this conclusion in the past tense?

Together with the eschatological ardor that runs through the letter—God has spoken "in these last days" (1:2) and expects believers to hold fast to their confession as they see "the Day approaching" (10:25)—it thus seems more likely that the author is writing before 70 CE than after. To be sure, this is a conclusion based partly on an argument from silence, but it is a telling silence that speaks volumes. Nevertheless, every day is the "today" of which the Holy Spirit speaks in Scripture, fervently addressing the contemporaries of Moses and of David with no less urgency than the readers of Hebrews (3:7–4:10). Whether the fact that Jesus Christ is "the same yesterday and today and forever" (13:8) would mitigate the hermeneutical importance of the letter's date or, like God, the author would have communicated "in many and various ways" depending on the time and season must remain an open question.

Occasion and purpose

There is no single precipitating event that compels the author to address the believers who saw fit to preserve Hebrews for posterity. They appear to be tempted to leave the fold they had joined when they "tasted the heavenly gift and shared in the Holy Spirit" (6:4) sometime earlier. The author's immediate concern is to prevent them from falling away and to encourage them to press on in the face of hostile treatment. Whether this mistreatment is at the hands of their neighbors or through more "official" channels, he does not say, presumably because they had no need to be reminded of the source. Instead of seeing in the author's message an alarm about apostasy manifesting itself in a return to the synagogue and the familiarity of its ritual practices, in the absence of polemic against false teachings or contemporary Jewish customs, it is perhaps more accurate to construe it as a warning against a creeping spiritual lethargy he fears has begun to take root. Or it may be that he is writing to a mixed audience that is beginning to wonder if the benefits of membership outweigh the liabilities. In either case, aligning themselves with a form of Jewish religion that enjoyed the status of a licit religion according to Roman law might relieve the social pressures to which they were being subjected. More importantly from the author's point of view, either of these dispositions would also pose a dire spiritual threat—"horizontally" to community solidarity and "vertically" to the access they enjoy to "the throne of grace" (4:16).

Such an impending crisis demands more than a generic pep talk. Nor will a dry theological disquisition fit the bill. The task has both practical and theoretical dimensions. They must be made to feel the gravity of their situation. They must also have a solid theological grounding for the author's exhortations, which the author supplies in the form of extended reflection on passages from the Old Testament (e.g., Gen. 14:18-20; Ps. 40:6-8; 95:7-11; 110; Jer. 31:31-34). Why should they remain faithful and not fall back? To this question his answer is emphatic: "Jesus has now obtained a more excellent ministry, and to that degree he is the mediator of a better covenant, which has been enacted through better promises. For if that first covenant had been faultless, there would have been no need to look for a second one" (8:6-7). Through his ministrations as high priest, Jesus justifies, sanctifies, writes the law on their hearts, and secures entry into the presence of their heavenly father now and at the hour of their death. The author therefore seeks to explain the ways in which the new covenant—God's distinctive way of dealing with humanity through Jesus—demands the utmost allegiance and remains perfectly consistent with the divine plan as disclosed under the original covenant.

Genre and structure

"Long ago," Hebrews begins, "God spoke to our ancestors in many and various ways" (1:1), and the Lord continues to speak in the present (1:1-2). With such an abiding interest in divine speech, it seems only fitting that the author is himself an accomplished wordsmith. He possesses a rich vocabulary and knows how to use it (Attridge 1989: 20–21). Well over a hundred words appear in Hebrews and nowhere else in the New Testament. Literary devices on display in the Greek text include alliteration (1:1; 4:16; 12:21), etymological wordplay (7:9; 9:16-17), anaphora (repetition of a word or phrase in successive clauses; for example, "by faith" throughout Hebrews 11), isocolon (a parallel structure in a sentence formed by two or more clauses of the same length: 1:3; 7:26), chiasm (an X-shaped sentence or argument organized according to an A-B-C-B'-A' pattern: 7:23-24; 10:38-39), and hyperbaton (inversion of the normal word order for the sake of emphasis: 2:9; 4:8).

All this is not literary artistry for its own sake but in the service of a sweeping argument about salvation history. The author of Hebrews deserves a place alongside Paul and John as the foremost theologian of the New Testament. But his work is by no means a systematic treatise. How, then, should it be classified? To the extent that it was sent from one individual to a specific audience, it qualifies as a letter. It is hardly a typical ancient letter, most notably in its opening but also in its length. In this respect, it resembles Paul's letter to the Romans and Seneca's letters to Lucilius. Its closing contains the standard elements found in the epistolary genre. It has been suggested that the final chapter has been added later to an essay or sermon that originally ended at Heb. 12:29. Thematic continuity and the lack of manuscript evidence to the contrary lead most scholars to regard Hebrews 13 as an integral part of the original text (Lane 1991: 495–507). Hebrews is a hybrid, then, more stylized than most letters and probably composed with the intent of having it delivered orally (cf. 2:5; 5:11; 8:1).

Hebrews refers to itself as a "word of exhortation" (13:22), a term used for Paul's brief sermon in Acts (13:15-41) in response to a request made by synagogue officials. Attempts to describe this genre highlight the use of examples drawn from Scripture and moral exhortation based on the application of these examples to the audience (Wills 1984). The focus on biblical examples leads others to see Hebrews as a series of midrashim, exercises in the interpretation of specific biblical texts in connection with a particular question or occasion. These two approaches share much in common, and their appeal is obvious in light of the author's repeated quotations from the Hebrew Bible (e.g., Ps. 2:7; 104:4; 45:6-7; 102:25-27; and 110:1 in Heb. 1:5-13; Ps. 8:4-6 in Heb. 2:5-18; Ps. 95:7-11 in Heb. 3:7–4:13; Ps. 110:4 in Heb. 5:1-10; Jer. 31:31-34 in Heb. 8:1–10:18). These elements can also be seen in Diaspora synagogue homilies, which have been analyzed with special attention to their reception aesthetics in the context of particular feast days on the Jewish liturgical calendar (e.g., Gelardini 2005). Surviving specimens of the word of exhortation, midrash, and the synagogue homily, not to mention early Christian letters, are too few and fragmentary as to permit hard and fast distinctions concerning their form and function. Like many other early Christian letters, Hebrews is both similar and dissimilar to these other genres, and relatively little interpretive leverage is to be had by attempting to fit it neatly into one or the other.

Disagreements over genre mask the larger consensus that Hebrews is a thoroughly rhetorical composition. Recently, it has become more common to analyze Hebrews in accordance with the well-documented canons of Greek and Roman rhetoric. Ancient handbooks such as those of Aristotle and Quintilian categorize speeches as either forensic (which seeks to persuade an audience to make judgments about past events), deliberative (which seeks to get an audience to choose a particular course of action in the future), or epideictic (which seeks to praise or blame a person, group, or idea). In its praise of Jesus in comparison with the angels (1:5-14), Moses (3:1-6), and Aaron and the Levitical priests (7:1-28), as well as in the litany of faithful ancestors in Hebrews 11, the letter functions epideictically. When he calls his readers to follow Jesus's example of perseverance (12:1-3), to strive for perfection (6:1-2), and to avoid apostasy (2:1-3; 6:4-6; 10:25-31), the author operates in a deliberative mode. Both the epideictic and the deliberative are present, and it is the former that can be seen in the expository sections and the latter in the hortatory sections.

The consistent alternation between biblical exposition and moral exhortation is one of the few structural aspects on which scholars agree. Wherever two or three scholars are gathered to discuss the structure of Hebrews in any detail, there are sure to be at least three or four different proposals. One leading approach maps the argument according to a chiastic scaffolding arranged around the central section in Heb. 5:11–10:39 devoted to Jesus's priestly office (Vanhoye 1989). The advantage of this proposal is in its close attention to transitions and "hook words," where the author concludes one section with a term that introduces a key theme in the following section, but one wonders whether an audience experiencing Hebrews aurally rather than on the written page would have noticed the intricate concentric patterns found in many commentaries.

Other commentators outline Hebrews according to the formal arrangements prescribed for ancient orators (Koester 2002). Speeches normally contained an *exordium* (introduction), *propositio* (thesis), *narratio* (the "facts" of the case), *probatio* ("proof" or argument), and *peroratio* (conclusion). Rhetorical analyses highlight the orderliness of the composition in terms that ancient authors themselves employed. Skilled speakers might make frequent creative departures from this template, however, such that it was perhaps more honored in the breach than the observance. It is the content—"invention" in the language of the Greco-Roman handbooks—and not the placement of the argument that matters more, and this aspect is the least reducible to a formula. It is not clear, moreover, what is learned by designating (according to the commentator) Hebrews 1 or 2 through Hebrews 10 or 12 as the argument, with what little remains as the introduction and conclusion.

As a general rule, the more complex the organizational scheme, the more precarious are the interpretations based on it. The commentary in the following pages pursues a more modest approach on structural questions, leaning in the direction of a thematic outline that attends to the textual dynamics uncovered by linguistic and rhetorical analyses and gives proper emphasis to the hortatory elements that may be overshadowed in an outline that privileges expository or "doctrinal" categories.

Outline

1

The Argument of Hebrews: God Speaks

The proclamation of the supremacy of Christ and his salvation (1:1–2:18)

From the outset, the exposition of Hebrews focuses on two vehicles of divine revelation: the Son and the Scriptures. Each conveys knowledge about the other. Having introduced the Son in just the second phrase, the author extols his supremacy throughout the first chapter in a series of citations from the sacred texts of the people of Israel. It is hardly remarkable for a first-century Christian writer to focus on Jesus and the Scriptures, but the author's exegetical twists and turns were, one may surmise, sufficiently provocative to hold the audience's attention.

The first sentence (vv. 1-4) in many modern translations comprises an entire paragraph. It includes no explicitly biblical material, but the author unmistakably echoes Scripture and thereby draws comparisons between the Son and various aspects of God, namely, God's word and God's wisdom. Several qualities are predicated of the Son in this opening sentence, many of which find parallels in the Old Testament. Hebrews may not refer to him as the *logos* ("word"), as does the prologue to the Gospel of John, but the Son is a medium of divine speech. Nor does Hebrews declare, like Paul, that Christ is "the wisdom of God" (1 Cor. 1:30), yet he exemplifies many of its signal qualities. God's powerful wisdom (Ps. 103:24; Prov. 3:19; Wis. 7:22, 27; 8:1) was active in the creation of the world, as was his word, to which the angels are said to be subservient (Ps. 32:6; Wis. 9:1; cf. Ps. 102:20). Wisdom also reflects God's glory and is associated with the name and greatness of God (Dan. 2:20; Wis. 7:25-26). Philo of Alexandria uses some of the same terminology as Heb. 1:3 in making many of the same attributions—for example, that wisdom existed before the beginning of time as the mother and nurse of the whole universe and that the word is the radiance (*apaugasma*) of the blessed nature and the seal (*charactēr*) of the divine nature (*Ebr.* 31; *Op. Mund.* 146 *Plant.* 18).

Two attributes of the Son are without precedent in Jewish descriptions of God's wisdom and word. First, Jewish writers never describe God's word or wisdom as an inheritor. People may inherit wisdom (Philo, *Heir* 98), but wisdom, as a personified quality, does not itself inherit anything. By contrast, in Hebrews, the Son is described as an heir at the beginning and end of the opening paragraph. Second, neither *Sophia* nor *Logos* are described as purifying agents.

By describing Jesus in this way, the author indicates that he finds widespread notions about the wisdom and word of God useful in understanding the Son without being constrained by them. In other words, the Son may be like God's word and God's wisdom, but he is not to be identified with either of them without remainder. He does things they do not do—namely, inherit and purify—which highlight his most important roles in Hebrews, Son and Priest. This opening paragraph shows the balance the author maintains between the old and the new. The old (the Scriptures) grants understanding of the new (the Son), but the new redefines the framework of the old. Hence, while the Scriptures convey knowledge about the Son, so too does the Son convey knowledge about the Scriptures.

This hermeneutical symbiosis becomes even more pronounced in the catena of seven Scripture citations in Heb. 1:5-13 (in order, Ps. 2:7; 2 Sam. 7:14; Deut. 32:43; Ps. 104:4; 45:6-7; 102:25-27; 110:1; cf. Schenck 2001). In some cases, the author has selected texts that in their original context refer to the heir of David. The first two citations fall into this category. Psalm 2:7 is a royal psalm that was read by some Jews as referring to the Messiah, as was 2 Sam. 7:14 (//1 Chron. 17:13), where Nathan speaks to David concerning his son. The fifth citation in vv. 8-9 (Ps. 45) is likewise written in praise of the king. The final citation (v. 13) from Ps. 110:1 is one of the most frequently cited messianic texts in the New Testament, so like other Jews who professed Jesus as the Messiah, this author saw such royal texts as applying to Jesus the Son.

The third and sixth texts in the catena refer to God rather than to David. In Deut. 32 (Heb. 1:6), Moses invites the angels to join him in praising God, and in Ps. 101:26-28 (Heb. 1:10-12) the psalmist acclaims God for his qualities of permanence and immutability. In the author's reading, texts about David and his son as well as texts about God apply to this Son. For this reason, Athanasius would later view the Son as fully divine and coequal with the Father. Arius cites the same texts to argue that he was a created being and therefore subordinate to the Father, with the "begetting" of the Son in Heb. 1:5 identified variously with Jesus's birth, baptism, death, resurrection, or exaltation. While the author of Hebrews might have felt out of place at Nicaea in 325 or Chalcedon in 451, in retrospect it is not difficult to see how the early church found in his writings a warrant for the dual assertion that Jesus was both a human heir of David and also worthy of worship as the eternal creator God.

Remarkably, the author does not make these claims on his own authority or in his own voice. This is a subtle but significant point. He does not simply claim that Scripture supports his claim about Jesus's messianic or divine status or even preface his quotations with the formula "it is written," as if he were engaged in a theological debate requiring the citation of sources. Instead, he retreats after his eloquent first sentence and allows God to speak. Each of the seven citations is introduced either explicitly or implicitly with "God said." Upon what greater authority could the author base his claims about this Son? Moreover, most of the citations (in vv. 5, 8-9, 10-12, and 13) take the form of direct address. God is speaking to the Son, and by presenting the texts in this way the author allows the audience to eavesdrop. No other New Testament author presents God's voice in quite the same manner (Docherty 2009).

If Hebrews had held the view that the age of prophecy had ceased— occasionally voiced in the postexilic period (1 Macc. 9:27; Josephus, *C. Ap.* 1.37-41; t. Soṭah 13.2)—its author now believes that any such hiatus is over. Moses, Nathan, Isaiah, Jeremiah, Habakkuk, and Haggai are among the prophets of old through whom people may hear God speaking in

Hebrews 1 and elsewhere in the letter. Against the view that God's voice has with time become more distant, muted, and difficult to distinguish, Hebrews asserts that it has never been transmitted with such clarity than "in these last days" (1:2).

But why do the angels appear in this thoroughly scriptural argument about the relationship between God and the Son in vv. 5-14? They serve as a foil to the Son in the first and last citation: God speaks in this way to the Son but never to angels. They give worship to the Son in the third citation and are described as ministering spirits and flames of fire in the fourth. In the final verse (v. 14) their role as servants to "those who are to inherit salvation" anticipates the discussion in Hebrews 2 of the relationship between the Son and his co-heirs, the other sons and daughters to whom Hebrews is addressed. Whether the angels are meant to represent a sort of ontological "buffer" between the divine and human that underscores the proximity of the Son to the former, as some interpreters have suggested, or to contrast with and thus accentuate the humanity of the Son is not clear (Bauckham 2008: 240–41). Whatever the precise significance, their presence facilitates the realization that, however mundanely orthodox Hebrews 1 may sound in its affirmation of the humanity and divinity of the Son, it was written by an author and for a community whose particular religious convictions and conceptual universe remain something of a mystery. Angels mattered then in a way that angels do not matter today for most readers, which serves as a reminder that even for many monotheistic communities the supernatural world is densely populated (cf. Heb. 12:22-24 to see how crowded "the heavenly Jerusalem" will be). Hebrews therefore invites readers to consider the known along with the unknown.

Here the angels appear in the first in a series of comparisons between Jesus and previous messengers and mediators. The author does not denigrate them or other precursors such as Moses (3:1-6) even as he stresses the auxiliary nature of their role in salvation history. The Son has appeared late in the game, so to speak, but it would be a mistake to consider his part as secondary or superfluous. With each comparison, the author concludes that Jesus is "better" or "superior." (The adjective *kreittōn* in Heb. 1:4—the Son has "become as much superior to angels as the name he has inherited is more excellent than theirs"—is used a dozen times in Hebrews.) The logic that governs the a fortiori argument that runs through Hebrews from beginning to end is premised on the validity of these prior announcements of God's will, a point to which the author turns in Hebrews 2.

The chapter division at this point makes perfect literary sense because for the first time (but not the last) the author moves from exegesis—his reading of Scripture—to exhortation—his charge concerning what actions the audience should take in light of the Scriptures explicated (2:1-4). Unsurprisingly for an orator of such skill, his first exhortation is that they pay close attention to what he has just told them, yet he includes himself in the group that should be listening, employing the first-person plural "we." To be sure, his own speech is worthy of a hearing, but more importantly, God's speech in the Scriptures and in the Son is to be heeded. Also for the first time, the author sounds a warning about the consequences that could result due to a lack of attention. Just as the mind wanders during a speech without concerted effort, so too might this audience drift away if they do not focus on God's words.

To emphasize the point, he returns to the angels. Jewish tradition sometimes held that angels were present at Mount Sinai and acted as intermediaries when God gave the law to Moses (*Jub.* 1.27-29; Josephus, *Ant.* 15.136; Acts 7:38). Transgression of God's word previously given through angels "received a just penalty," the author reminds them, and any disregard for God's word more recently delivered through the Son will likewise be punished (2:2-3). There is some ambiguity in the way he describes the harm in "neglect[ing] so great a salvation." The expected answer to his rhetorical question ("how can we escape?") is obviously, "we cannot." This may imply that there can be no escape from God's punishment or, alternatively, that there can be no escape from the situation in which humanity finds itself— that is, enslaved to the fear of death (cf. 2:15). In other words, it might be not that God actively punishes those who do not heed his salvific word in the Son, but in so doing, they leave themselves in thrall to "the one who has the power of death, that is, the devil" (2:14). Whereas sins of commission were punished in the past, "in these last days" a sin of omission may lead to even more dire consequences. Both the promise and the peril are now higher than in the past, and so the audience must attend to the good news even more diligently if they are not to be "among those who shrink back and so are lost" (10:39).

The author goes into further detail concerning the manner in which God has now communicated this great salvation. A three-step process begins with the salvation being spoken by the Lord. First, *kyrios* can refer either to God or to Jesus in other New Testament writings, but because the author of Hebrews has previously used it exclusively in reference to the Son (Heb. 1:10) and because this message is then passed on by people who heard him, it makes sense to understand "Lord" in Heb. 2:3 as a reference to the speech of the human Jesus. The second step involves the messengers. They communicate this salvation from the Lord to the author and his audience. Finally, God supplements their witness, not through the medium of words but of deeds, including "wonders and various miracles, and by gifts of the Holy Spirit" (2:4). The author articulates no fully developed Trinitarian theology, but all three "persons" of God, as they will later be known, are involved here in the dissemination of this salvific revelation.

After this first exhortation, the author resumes his exegesis in Heb. 2:5-9, again drawing a comparison with angels. But in contrast to Hebrews 1, here Jesus's sovereignty over the angels derives not from his status as Son of God, but as "son of man." The author interprets portions of a psalm praising God for caring for humanity (Ps. 8:4-6) in reference to Jesus. By rendering *huios anthrōpou* as "mortals" or "human beings" (NRSV; CEB) rather than "son of man," some translations completely obscure the unmistakable allusion to Jesus that the author finds in the literal words of the Septuagint text he is quoting. The translation of singular pronouns ("him," "his") as plural ("them," "their") has the same distorting effect. Jesus is the one who was made lower than the angels and is now crowned with glory and honor. The author understands *brachy* (vv. 7, 9) temporally rather than spatially (so, in English, "for a little while"), in line with his emphasis on the work accomplished by Jesus's suffering during his time on earth. In this respect, the narrative of Jesus's career resembles that of the "Christ hymn" quoted by Paul in Phil. 2:6-11. As Jews looked forward to the day when humans would reign over God's creation, Jesus is now the first human to exercise that sovereignty (cf. 1QS 4:22b-23a; *Jub.* 1:29; 4 Ezra 7:10-14; Moffitt 2011: 81–118). By virtue of his relationship both with God and with humanity, Jesus is supreme over the angels.

Hebrews now has more to say about the Son's relationship with humanity and the significance of the suffering he experiences in that state (2:10-13). The author claims that suffering worked to bring him to "perfection." Moreover, this suffering has salvific merit for the many children who are on their way to glory because the perfected Jesus serves as "the pioneer of their salvation" (2:10; cf. 12:2). The notion of vicarious suffering raises eyebrows among some feminist theologians, but the potential difficulty is further heightened when the author says that God's involvement is "fitting." Does Hebrews advocate a kind of cosmic child abuse by which the Father inflicts suffering upon the Son (Brown and Bohn 1989)? Two factors suggest that the answer is no: (1) according to Hebrews, the Father allows this suffering but does not inflict it. Rather, its true sources are sin and the devil; and (2) the Son willingly takes on the suffering of death out of his own desire to rescue humanity.

The author's primary focus is on the way in which this process sets humanity into a specific relationship. "The one who sanctifies and those who are sanctified" come from one source (literally, "are all of one"). Both Adam and God have been identified as this unnamed source, but by this point in the letter, it is clear that neither one can be denied. Jesus and his followers share both the human condition and also God as their father. By virtue then of his dual sonships—he is son of humanity as well as Son of God—he is unashamed to address humanity as his siblings. He has been lowered to the human condition and so shares their humanity, and he has in turn elevated them into a relationship in which God is their father.

Of the many prooftexts he might have chosen, why does the author make his case by invoking Ps. 21:23 LXX in Heb. 2:12-13? The initial motivation, it seems, is to put a text on the Son's lips in which he uses the word *adelphos*, "brother." This citation is taken from a later portion of the same psalm which, in Matthew and Mark, supplies Jesus's last words from the cross (Ps. 22:1 in Mt. 27:46; Mk 15:34: "My God, my God, why have you forsaken me?"). The verse quoted in Hebrews comes from a later section where the psalmist turns from lament to praise. Jesus also addresses God as he declares that humans are his siblings. If Jesus is the "firstborn" Son of God (Rom. 8:29; Col. 1:15; Rev. 1:5) and believers are, here as elsewhere in early Christian discourse, children of God (Jn 1:12; Rom. 8:14-17; Gal. 4:6-7), then it follows that he is their older brother, setting a far better example in this role than Cain and Esau, the other older brothers mentioned in Hebrews (11:4; 12:16-17).

One might read these citations as the second half of a conversation that began in Hebrews 1, with the Son now replying to the Father. Here Jesus vows to praise and trust God and to proclaim his name "to [his] brothers and sisters." One can imagine Jesus proudly pointing to these siblings as he speaks the words of the citation from Isa. 8:18. The motif of Jesus acknowledging that God has entrusted to him those he will save is found also in the "high priestly prayer" of the Fourth Gospel (Jn 17:2, 10). The author has Jesus proclaim what he wants his audience to embody—continued trust in God—and it is on this basis that "he is not ashamed to call them brothers and sisters" (2:11).

In Heb. 2:14-18, the author restates his affirmation of the Son's humanity and draws out its soteriological significance. Since his siblings shared in flesh and blood, he took on the same nature (though see the later qualification in 4:15 that he became like humans in every respect "yet without sin"). At this point, it becomes clear why his death makes a difference for others. His death has consequences that reverberate not only in this world, where humans are "all their lives . . . held in slavery by the fear of death," but also in the world above and the world below as well. Very few texts in the New Testament so unambiguously espouse the *Christus Victor* theory of the atonement as Heb. 2:14-15. Only by assuming flesh and blood and tasting death for everyone could Jesus destroy the devil and the fear of death he inspires. The devil is here identified as one of the enemies that God has promised to put under the feet of the Son (1:13), even if his final rescue of humanity still lies in the future. His death has nevertheless struck the decisive blow and set in motion the events that will culminate in a cosmic victory. Given that Heracles is the "pioneer" (*archēgos*) to whom Jesus is most often compared in the secondary literature and even by ancient readers like Justin Martyr and Celsus, the efficacy of his weakness is striking (cf. Aune 1990).

The final sentences of Hebrews 2 specify that the aid given by Jesus is for "the descendants of Abraham" and not angels. There is no indication that deliverance from fear of death is applicable only to those who are Jews by physical descent. Rather, the contrast with angels is intended to accentuate their humanity. While the audience might conceivably consist exclusively of Jewish believers, "Abraham's seed" here may simply denote anyone who professes faith in Christ, as it frequently does in Paul's letters (Rom. 4:16-17; 9:6-8; Gal. 3:6-9, 14, 29). His humanity is a prerequisite for the office of "merciful and faithful high priest in service to God" (2:17). This is the first appearance of the dominant Christological motif by which the author delineates the superiority of the new covenant over the old. The peculiar nature of this priesthood, its blueprint in the Jewish Scriptures, its relationship to his messianic and filial identity, and its implications for the audience are elucidated in later sections of the letter (esp. 5:1-10:18).

The example of Israel in the wilderness (3:1–4:13)

The "heavenly calling" in which the readers are "holy partners" is Jesus's priestly intercession introduced in the last few verses of Hebrews 2 (3:1). Whether they are eventually to assume duties similar to those discharged by Jesus is not stated, but the author repeatedly reminds them they are destined to take their place in heaven (4:14-16; 10:19-25; 11:16; 12:22-25). "Apostle" is added to the title of high priest, neither of which is applied to Jesus elsewhere in the New Testament. A symmetry in this dual appellation is to be found in the status of an apostle as one sent by God with a mission and the function of a priest to represent the people in responding to God, and together these titles express the author's understanding of Jesus's role as "mediator" (Johnson 2006: 106–7).

Moses here makes his first of many appearances in Hebrews (3:1-6; cf. 7:14; 8:5; 9:19; 10:28; 11:23-24; 12:21). The context for the comparison with Jesus is an allusion to Num. 12:7 LXX, where God defends Moses against the complaints of Aaron and Miriam that he has compromised his own standing as a prophet by marrying a Cushite woman. God affirms the superiority of Moses, with whom he speaks "face to face" and not through dreams and visions. This episode may have appealed to the author of Hebrews in that it supplies one more example of the variability of divine speech. Some divine communications resound with greater clarity than others, as he suggests in the letter's opening verses. Both Moses and Jesus are "faithful in all God's house." Moses is faithful as a "servant," but this is intended to highlight his humble trust in God rather than to denigrate his prophetic calling. Nor is this terminology necessarily intended to remind readers that Moses remains enslaved to the fear of death (2:15; instead of *doulos*, "slave" here renders *therapōn*, which can refer to a free person who has freely entered the service of a superior and often enjoys a position of honor). Nevertheless, in the hierarchy of intermediaries who serve God, Hebrews places Moses below Jesus, who was "faithful over God's house as a son." Later in Hebrews, critique of the Levitical priesthood will be more pointed than what one finds here. However mild the contrast may seem, there is a sense that any course of action indicating a preference for Moses as a patron would be to forego the greater privileges they enjoy by virtue of their identity as the siblings of Jesus in God's household (*oikos*). This is the basis for the "confidence" they should possess, not as a subjective feeling or emotion but as an objective reality that can be grasped by considering both the positive and negative examples furnished by Scripture.

As a negative example, Heb. 3:7–4:11 presents the members of the exodus generation who followed Moses in the desert for forty years. Along with the citation of Jer. 31:31-34 in Hebrews 8, this is one of the longest citations of an Old Testament passage in any New Testament book. This transition constitutes a slight mixing of metaphors in that the "house" in which Moses and Jesus act as servant and son is an ordinary household while the focus of the rest of Hebrews 3 is the house of Israel. The excerpt from the psalm quoted here (95:7-11 LXX) alludes to the rebellions at Meribah and Massah, where the Israelites quarrel with Moses and Aaron for leading them into the desert where they have no water. Following the LXX, Hebrews translates these place names, which mean "rebellion" and "testing," rather than simply transliterating them as proper nouns and thereby accentuates the paradigmatic role they serve in his exposition (Koester 2001: 264). The inclusion of Joshua in his analysis in Heb. 4:8 may indicate that the author is conflating these episodes (Exod. 17:1-7; Num. 20:1-13) with a separate episode in Num. 14:1-12 where God threatens to disinherit the people in anger at their disbelief in spite of the great deeds he has performed on their behalf.

Notwithstanding the barriers of time and space, the author sees in the experience of the Israelites a clear testimony that God's word confronts believers at all times and places with the same immediacy. Speaking through the psalmist, the Holy Spirit directs to the audience the same warning about the consequences of disobedience. Hebrews relies on the Septuagint rendering of the quotation by phrasing the initial clause as a conditional ("if you hear his voice") unlike the more plaintive wish expressed in the Hebrew text (RSV: "O that today you would hearken to his voice!"). The author's syntax also diverges from both the Hebrew and the Greek in vv. 9-10, with the result that the Israelites are said to have witnessed God's work for forty years rather than enduring his wrath for forty years. In calling on the audience to "hear his voice"—an admonition he repeats twice more (3:15; 4:7)—he retains the connotation of the Hebrew verb *shāma*; to hear is to obey. "Obedience" (*hypakoē*) in Greek likewise shares a root with "hearing" (*akoē*). The physical wandering chronicled in Torah is paralleled by the spiritual wandering of the audience. Forty years is a long time for such a journey, especially when one looks at the map and remembers that the Sinai peninsula is actually quite small. (It is tempting but inconclusive to conjecture that the author is in part motivated to draw this particular parallel because he is writing in or about 70 CE, forty years after the death of Jesus.) This aimlessness accounts for the lack of progress in the faith for which the author chides his audience in Heb. 5:11-14.

Hebrews is not alone in mining the time spent in the wilderness for spiritual instruction (Steyn 2011: 173–75). Biblical and non-biblical sources highlight the sins of the ancestors and counsel their descendants in various periods to take heed lest they repeat them. God's wrath and the blasphemies of the people are held up as object lessons by, among others, Ezekiel (20:1-31) and the members of the Qumran community (CD 3:7-13). Paul cites a different episode in 1 Cor. 10: 1-13 but makes explicit the hermeneutical perspective he shares with Hebrews when he says that "these things occurred as examples for us, so that we might not desire evil as they did." The waywardness of the Israelites is certainly lamentable, but the author's application of this narrative to the situation of his audience suggests that he regards the peril they face to be even greater. "They always go astray [planōntai] in their hearts," according to the quotation within the quotation of Ps. 95:10 LXX in v. 10. When he begins his own commentary on the psalm in v. 12, he says to take care that none of them have "an evil, unbelieving heart that turns away [apostēnai] from the living God." From "going astray" to "turning away," the author has opted for language that portrays their present trajectory as a more serious departure, even if the failure of the Israelites to "know [God's] ways" qualified as culpable ignorance.

Apostasy is here described as turning away from "the living God," before whom they will ultimately stand and face judgment (10:26-31; 12:22-23). It rarely takes the form of a deliberate renunciation of a previous oath or profession of faith. No one sets out consciously intending to cultivate a "hardened" heart. Rather, it is often the case that a person drifts slowly, almost imperceptibly, gathering inertia until reaching a point from which it is difficult to return. For this reason, it is important for them "to exhort one another every day," so as to prevent bad spiritual habits from developing into a settled disposition. Their mutual exhortation must continue "as long as it is called 'today,'" because there may come a day when, the author hints, God's patience is exhausted. Only by persevering "to the end" will they avoid learning what the Israelites learned "in the rebellion" (3:13-15).

For now, "the promise of entering his rest" remains open (4:1-11). "Rest" (katapausis) signifies three different realities in Hebrews. (1) The author connects the psalm to Gen. 2:2 and God's rest on the seventh day of creation. Jewish tradition commemorates God's completion of the work of creation in the observance of the Sabbath. (2) Settlement in the land of Canaan was promised by God (Deut. 12:9) and was anticipated after forty years in the desert. (3) Heaven is the final goal of the believer (11:13-16; 12:22-24). This understanding of rest is correlated with the description of life as a pilgrimage in Hebrews 11–12. Later references to persecution also suggest that there is a qualitative and not just a temporal dimension to the rest promised to the audience. In this respect, if they do not regard their present difficulties as divine judgment, they may proleptically experience some measure of relief in advance of the eschaton (4:10-11). The author interprets this rest as one form in which they may expect the fulfillment of God's "promise," a pervasive theme in Hebrews (6:12-15, 17; 7:6; 8:6; 9:15; 10:23, 36; 11:9, 11, 13, 17, 33, 39; 12:26).

God's wrath is reserved for those who do not enter this rest. Having reassured the audience that they have grounds for confidence (*parrēsia*) as siblings of Jesus in Heb. 3:6, the author reminds them that they have good reason for fear should they turn back. "Take care" (NIV; NRSV) is thus too tepid for the subjunctive *phobēthōmen* in Heb. 4:1, which the RSV appropriately renders "let us fear." He goes back and forth between rhetorically dangling the carrot and wielding the stick. In the repeated term "today" (*sēmeron*) and in the biblical chronology, he finds an opening through which he can extend an invitation to respond in faith. Reasoning that David would not have spoken as he does in the Psalms had the book been closed on the matter in Joshua's day, he infers that every day is the "today" spoken in Scriptures. Joshua was not able to provide the rest they sought, but he impressed on his own generation the necessity of deciding "today" (*sēmeron* in Josh. 24:15 LXX) whom they would serve, as did his predecessor Moses throughout Deuteronomy (2:25; 4:8, 39-40; 5:1; 6:6; 7:11; 8:1; 11:2; 13:18; 15:5; 19:9; 26:16; 29:12-28; 30:15). Interestingly, Hebrews underscores this point by overlooking texts (e.g., Josh. 21:43-45; 1 Kgs 8:56) which state that God did in fact grant the Israelites "rest" at the end of their sojourn (Thiessen 2007: 355–56). Dragging their feet, the author seems to warn, will only cause them to lose the opportunity to turn to God, not unlike Esau in Heb. 12:17. Although the compilers of the Mishnah do not rely on Hebrews, the urgency of "today" later becomes associated with repentance in rabbinic traditions in a way that will recapitulate many of the motifs found in Hebrews 3–4 (Flusser 1988: 59).

One aspect of the lesson Hebrews draws from this episode adds a layer of nuance to its teaching on faith. Comparisons of Hebrews with Paul on this point are sometimes oversimplified but can also bring their respective teachings into sharper relief. An emphasis on the element of radical trust "in Christ" has been central to understandings of faith informed by Martin Luther's reading of Romans and Galatians. In contrast, faith in Hebrews is often seen as a form of faithfulness that, insofar as it is located in or exercised by the believer, can resemble a form of obedience with which it is incommensurate in the view of Protestant interpreters who hold up the Pauline doctrine as normative. The ambiguity is due in part to the fact that the adjective *pistos* can mean either trusting ("believing in") or trustworthiness (that is, worthy of one's trust or belief). However much this construal may overlook inconvenient texts in Paul's letters—for example, his desire to bring about "the obedience of faith" in Rom. 1:5—it cannot be denied that faith and obedience are closely related in passages such as Heb. 3:7–4:11, where language associated with both concepts is used interchangeably. Woe to them if they have an "unbelieving heart" that turns away from God, as did many of the Israelites (3:12). God had sworn "to the disobedient" that they would not enter his rest (3:18). Lest the audience misunderstand, the author immediately adds that those "whose bodies fell in the wilderness . . . were unable to enter because of unbelief" (3:17, 19), only to substitute "disobedience" for "unbelief" twice more in otherwise parallel phrases before the end of the section (4:6, 11). Given its pairing with disobedience, it is perhaps better to render *apistia* as "faithlessness" instead of the milder "unbelief." The good news might not benefit their ancestors "because they were not united by faith with those who listened," but "we who have believed enter that rest" (4:2-3).

At the conclusion of the citation of Ps. 95:7-11, the author punctuates his commentary with a vivid assertion that Scripture is much more than a passive repository of Israelite traditions worthy of his audience's attention (4:12-13). "The word of God is living and active," he says, "sharper than any two-edged sword" from which nothing is kept secret. The root of the verb the NRSV renders "laid bare" can refer to the bending back of the neck of a sacrificial victim before its throat is slit (Diogenes Laertius 6.61), which complements the description of Scripture's capacity to "divide soul from spirit, joints from marrow" and underscores for the audience the urgency of responding in faith "today" when the spirit speaks.

Jesus the great high priest (4:14–5:10)

The commentary on the wilderness generation in Heb. 3:7–4:11 concludes with a warning about disobedience and a sobering comment that there will be a final reckoning with the one who is "able to judge the thoughts and intentions of the heart" and from whom nothing is hidden (4:12-13). In the following section, the author assumes a more reassuring tone when he finally turns his full attention to Jesus's role as priest after alluding to it earlier (1:3; 3:1; 2:17), reminding his readers that they have good reason for confidence to approach the throne of grace (4:16). This is not to say that the author has exhausted the topic of Jesus's identity as Son. Quite to the contrary, in this initial treatment of priesthood, Jesus's dual sonships—he is both Son of God (4:14; 6:6) and son of humanity (2:6)—qualify him for his priestly calling.

Divine and human qualities are on display in ways that are sometimes difficult to distinguish in the author's thought (4:14-15). Jesus resides where God resides since he has "passed through the heavens" yet is able to sympathize with human weakness. He has been tested "in every respect . . . as we are," yet remains completely untainted by sin. His humanity and the manner in which it illustrates his fitness as high priest is accentuated by a comparison with Aaron and others "chosen from among mortals" (5:1-4). By joining a psalm (2:7) that identifies Jesus as God's son with another (110:4) that specifies his priesthood as one that lasts forever, Hebrews signals that "the order of Melchizedek" is a priesthood unlike any other (Hay 1973: 114–45). This is the first mention of the enigmatic figure whose appearances in the Old Testament are limited to Gen. 14:18-20 and Ps. 110:4. No other New Testament writer mentions him or characterizes Jesus as a priest. This Christological affirmation is unique to the author of Hebrews, who will later expand on it at length (7:1-28).

From the list of priestly qualifications and duties associated with Aaron and the Levites, the author focuses on the intensely human experience of suffering Jesus undergoes (5:5-10). Hebrews manifests arguably the "lowest" Christology in the New Testament in this passage a few chapters after what is arguably, alongside the Fourth Gospel, its highest Christological formulation in the opening chapter. He faces death "in the days of his flesh," not stoically, but with emotion, crying out in trust to God who could deliver him from death. The description calls to mind the demeanor of the pious supplicant in Hellenistic Judaism, though with language ("loud cries and tears") that can also be used for the squealing of pigs or dogs (*Barn.* 10.3), the portrayal of Jesus is almost subhuman.

Many interpreters believe that the author has in mind the prayer of Jesus in Gethsemane that the cup of suffering be removed from his lips if it is God's will (Mt. 26:36-46; Mk 14:32-42; Lk. 22:29-46). To focus exclusively on Gethsemane as the setting for Jesus's prayer as envisioned by Hebrews is not necessary, especially in light of the possibility that the letter was written earlier than the Gospels, though the author may have been familiar with oral traditions related to the episode. Alternatively, it has been suggested that when he prays in v. 7 "to the one who was able to save him from death," Hebrews understands Jesus to be not in the garden but on the cross

(Swetnam 2000: 356–60). Similarities with Psalm 22 support this reading. Beginning with the cry of dereliction, "My God, my God, why have you forsaken me?" this psalm is on Jesus's tongue in the Synoptic accounts of the crucifixion and is quoted in several other New Testament texts, including Heb. 2:12 (cf. Jn 19:24; 1 Pet. 5:8). When the psalmist declares (22:25), "The Lord has not turned his face from me, and when I cried to him, he heard me," it is not difficult to imagine the author finding it congenial to his Christological agenda in Heb. 5:7-8.

But what, exactly, is the content of Jesus's prayer? Especially if one views Gethsemane as the setting Hebrews presupposes, then it follows that a prayer "to the one who was able to save him from death [*ek thanatou*]" would have as its goal the avoidance of death. Jesus's eventual death causes difficulties for this interpretation, however, to the extent that his prayer is "heard." Could it be, rather, that Jesus actually asks not to avoid death but to be allowed to die? In this case, he gets precisely what he asks for. One may also construe "from death" in spatial terms, that is, that God answers Jesus's prayers by raising him "out of" death. In early Christian parlance, this would appear to be an allusion to the resurrection. Hebrews emphasizes exaltation more than resurrection in its account of Jesus's post-Calvary ministry. References to resurrection are few, and only in the final benediction (13:20-21) is the rising of Jesus unambiguously in view. The resurrection therefore constitutes the divine response to Jesus's prayer. Far from being peripheral to the narrative substructure of the author's thought, then, the resurrection is central to his theology (Moffitt 2011). According to Hebrews, the "perfection" that qualifies Jesus for priesthood requires his resurrection to "an indestructible life" (5:9-10; 7:16).

In asking to be raised from the dead, Jesus would in essence be acquiescing in his own death. It does not detract from the humanity the author assigns to Jesus to portray him as hoping for and firmly believing that he would be raised from the dead. He experiences fear—not the abject terror that might be implied by *phobos*, but a reasonable apprehension in the face of a truly adverse state of affairs, together with a worshipful attentiveness to God's will. *Eulabeia* in v. 8 bears this sense, and it is translated variously as "reverent submission" (NRSV) or "godly fear" (RSV). This fear is only one aspect of "what he suffered," which in turn was the means by which he "learned obedience" (5:8). That learning comes through suffering was a widespread aphorism in the Greco-Roman world. Jesus's own "education" yields much more than hard-won wisdom for a fulfilling life. His "perfection" in v. 9 benefits his followers by creating the conditions for their salvation.

Paradoxically, Hebrews seems to imply that Jesus has become more fully human than any other human and that his perfection therefore subsists, to some degree, in his susceptibility to weakness and imperfection.

The structure of this initial discussion of Jesus's priestly role thus begins with his distinctively divine qualities, centers around his similarities with other priests, and concludes with the inescapable reality of his human experience. He is a priest like others, but in both the heights to which he rises and the depths to which he descends, his experience with God and the human condition fits him to be a priest par excellence. An element of paradox seems unavoidable. Insofar as there is nothing unusual in the need for an ordinary son to learn obedience, this characterization implicitly underscores the divine qualities borne by Jesus. Even though he is the kind of son that he is, he still learns.

This unique priesthood, likewise, has unparalleled implications for those who follow him. They can boldly approach God's throne confident that they will receive mercy, grace, and help at just the right time (4:16). Hebrews never refers to Jesus as "savior" (*sōter*), but his use of *sōtēria* in reference to the assistance received by the believer through his death here and throughout the letter (e.g., 1:14; 2:10; 6:9; 9:28) means that Jesus merits this title. "Having been made perfect," the author boldly states, "he became the source of eternal salvation for all who obey him" (5:9). Soteriologically and Christologically, this is a more robust claim than one finds with interpreters who essentially ignore the final clause or gloss this verse as a generic call to imitate Jesus. Obedience is owed to God or to the law, and thus to understand Jesus's role as purely or primarily exemplary in nature fails to do justice to the author's provocative argument. By portraying him as one fit to command obedience and endow the faithful with supernatural blessings yet willing to "deal gently" with them on account of his own susceptibility to weakness (5:2), the author blurs the distinction between the divine and the human in the person of Jesus.

Christian maturity: Warnings and encouragement (5:11–6:20)

At the mention of Melchizedek's name in Heb. 5:10, the author realizes he has "much to say that is hard to explain" and puts off this exegetical heavy lifting for a few paragraphs. A pause is necessary if, as he senses, his readers are not up to the challenge. Their dullness may be a function of their reluctance to follow in Jesus's footsteps in "learning obedience" through suffering (Johnson 2006: 154–55). To prepare them for the "solid food" he will serve in Hebrews 7, he first chides them for their immaturity (5:11-14), invites them to consider the consequences of a failure to heed God's word (6:1-8), and then offers encouragement from their own past and from God's record of fidelity (6:9-20).

From this transition one learns that the recipients of the letter have confessed Christ for long enough that they should have already become teachers. Training as a teacher in the Jewish synagogue or as a tutor in the Greco-Roman educational system took considerable time. They are not neophytes. Their lack of progress, then, is for the author a worrisome sign of spiritual lethargy (cf. 6:10). More than simply losing momentum, he fears they may have regressed given that they still need to review certain fundamental teachings ("the basic elements of the oracles [*logia*] of God"). Like infants, they are "unskilled in the word of righteousness." He then adds a common jab: they need milk, not solid food, which is only fit for the "mature" (*teleioi*), that is, "those whose faculties have been trained by practice [*hexis*] to distinguish good from evil." His diagnosis corresponds with descriptions of the moral life found among Greek philosophers (e.g., Aristotle, *Eth. Nic.* 2.1.1-8) who see all human activity as driving toward a *telos* ("end" or "purpose") and who uses *hexis* to denote the character that results from habits (Lee 1997: 158–59). More importantly, his critique registers at both the natural and supernatural levels. They have not paid proper attention to God's word nor have they correctly apprehended the good and evil in the world around them.

This hiatus in the argument is temporary, and the author intends to press on to the advanced curriculum (6:1-3). His comments here may be aspirational, however, insofar as he never completely "leaves behind the basic teachings about Christ": he will continue to teach them about repentance and faith (6:4-6; 11:1-40), his warnings all focus on eternal judgment (9:27; 10:26-31), and the final blessing highlights the resurrection from the dead (13:20-21). His concern that they may be "carried away by all kinds of strange teachings" never quite disappears (13:9). But he pauses again to consider the question of apostasy because, before he can address a topic for the mature like Christ's priesthood "according to the order of Melchizedek," he warns them of the dangers of immaturity. It is not just lack of growth or stagnation that frustrates him. The possibility of regression, of falling away, compels him to issue the grave warning found in Heb. 6:4-8.

Herein lies one of the conundrums of Hebrews: Does its author believe that genuine followers of Jesus the Messiah can forfeit the relationship they have with God? It is certainly possible to read Heb. 6:4-8 as supporting this notion. This is perhaps the most vigorously contested passage in the entire letter, having sparked debate from the second century up to the present (Nicole 1975). The author declares:

> For it is impossible to restore again to repentance those who have once been enlightened, and have tasted the heavenly gift, and have shared in the Holy Spirit, and have tasted the goodness of the word of God and the powers of the age to come, and then have fallen away, since on their own they are crucifying again the Son of God and are holding him up to contempt. (vv. 4-6)

"Enlightenment" here is almost certainly a metaphor for baptism and hence an allusion to their conversion (Eph. 5:14; 1 Pet. 2:9; Justin Martyr, *Apol.* 1.61). This passage has been read as disallowing repentance for any and all post-baptismal sin, especially among Novatianists in the third century, though most interpreters believe that here and in Heb. 10:26 the author most likely has intentional apostasy in mind. Even in this "softer" reading, does *adynaton* mean "impossible" or only, by hyperbole, "very difficult," perhaps in light of eschatological exigencies that would leave insufficient time for (re)turning (*metanoia* can mean "repentance" or "conversion")? The author describes these people as those who have tasted (*geuomai*) of various heavenly realities. "Tasting" is how Jesus experiences death (2:9), thus the author uses the term here to connote something deeper than mere intellectual assent. Moreover, he says that they are *metochoi* of the Holy Spirit. God gave the Holy Spirit to those who heard the message of salvation (2:4), and the author uses *metochoi* for partners of Jesus or participants in his calling (1:9; 3:1, 14; 12:8). The rhetorical force of this series of descriptive clauses makes it evident that the author is describing individuals who have joined the fold and not simply received forgiveness for sins upon expressing remorse.

If it is the case that the author is describing members of the community who have pledged their allegiance to Jesus, then he also seems to believe it is possible for them to fall away (6:6). If they apostatize, then it is impossible to renew them to repentance because they would have to crucify for themselves the Son of God and hold him up to mockery all over again. The participle *anastaurountas* is ambiguous; it may mean merely "crucifying" or "crucifying again," as the prefix *ana-* frequently indicates repetition. Notwithstanding the prevailing use of the verb to mean "crucify" without the element of repetition, the Vulgate and many ancient and modern interpreters opt for the latter reading. (There was little need for a special term to denote crucifying a person a second time if only because the technology was sufficiently advanced to do the job on the first try.) Recrucifying parallels the phrase "restore again" in v. 4 and complements the emphasis on the once-for-all efficacy of Jesus's sacrificial death. For Hebrews, the motif expresses the logic of Jesus's death in the form of an argument ad absurdum: the cross was a singular event, therefore the problem of sin it was intended to solve must not be repeated. (Note, however, the reply of Jesus, whom Peter encounters in the *Acts of Peter* as he leaves Rome to avoid persecution. When Peter asks, "Where are you going [*Quo vadis*]?" Jesus says, "Yes, *again* shall I be crucified.")

The author of Hebrews is not exactly asking, "Can a Christian lose his or her salvation?" Instead, he is thinking through potential consequences of "immaturity": lack of discernment, remediation in the "basics," inability to produce good fruit, in which case they are "worthless and on the verge of being cursed" (6:8). Faith cannot stand still or it will fester and die. For Hebrews, standing still is tantamount to turning back. Should one disregard Christ's sacrifice on the cross, the hope of salvation would appear to be gone since this one-time act cannot be repeated.

He has described for his readers a terrifying path that lies uncomfortably open for traffic, but they have not yet traveled so far down it that a change of direction cannot be made (6:9-12). Even though his tone has been stern, he remains convinced that this congregation he loves is on the road to salvation. His confidence rests in the fact that their faith has resulted in good works, namely, their continuing service toward the other saints, and his earnest desire is that they "continue to show the same diligence so as to realize the full assurance of hope to the very end." With the mention of the "end" (*telos*) and the caution against sluggishness (*nōthroi*) in vv. 11-12, he returns to where the warning began (5:11).

A positive example now comes into view—Abraham, who did not give up on trusting God and, in remaining faithful, "inherited the promises" (6:13-20). There were times when Abraham's trust may appear to have waned, but the author focuses on the statement in Gen. 22:17 after Abraham demonstrates his trust most fully when tested by God. The initiative here lies not with Abraham, even when he is willing to sacrifice (cf. Heb. 11:17-19), but with God who "desired to show even more clearly to the heirs of the promise the unchangeable character of his purpose." God makes the promise,

God swears, God blesses, God multiplies, God guarantees. Abraham's story is an important example but only inasmuch as it is an occasion to remind the readers of the faithfulness of God. The source of their hope is God's steadfastness. As heirs to the promise made to Abraham, it is imperative that they remain true to their baptismal vow.

Having provided this encouragement, the author may now return to the subject he wanted to broach a chapter ago, that is, the way in which Melchizedek and his priesthood prefigures the intercession in heaven made by Jesus, "a forerunner on our behalf."

2

The Argument of Hebrews: Priesthood and Covenant

Jesus and Melchizedek (7:1-28)

The introduction of Melchizedek in connection with Jesus's high priesthood occurs in Heb. 5:1-10. One suspects that this is what the author has in mind when he says he has "much that is hard to explain" (5:11). His explanation in Hebrews 7 is longer and more detailed than the rest of the biblical testimony concerning Melchizedek combined. He is of interest to the author because of the invocation of his name in Ps. 110. Whereas this psalm is a popular messianic prooftext among early Christian writers (e.g., Lk. 20:42; Acts 2:24; 1 Cor. 15:25; Col. 3:1), Hebrews alone dwells on the reference to Melchizedek. His only other appearance in the Hebrew Scriptures, Gen. 14:17-20, is a brief cameo interjected in the Abraham cycle. For modern readers, the comparison of Jesus and Melchizedek is perhaps the oddest aspect of the author's entire argument. Ancient readers were also captivated by this mysterious figure (Horton 1976). The Dead Sea Scrolls and other Jewish literature ascribe to him various divine or angelic attributes and give him a role in the end times (1QapGen 22; 11QMelch; 2 En. 69–74).

Philo offers an etymology for his name that attempts to clarify his status as a priest-king (*Leg. All.* 79–82; cf. Josephus, *Ant.* 180; Hebrews's translation of *malchi*, *tzedek*, and *salēm* in v. 2 may indicate that some portion of the audience needed a Greek translation). Rabbinic writings (*Lev. Rab.* 25:6) identify him as Noah's son Shem and speculate that he taught Torah to Abraham long before Moses received the law. The fleeting nature of the Genesis narrative, with so little obvious relationship to Jesus, suggests that it was not the primary impetus of the author's Christological exposition. Rather, it seems likely that an antecedent understanding of Jesus's death as a sacrifice gave rise to the corollary that Jesus was in some sense a priest, which in turn sent the author of Hebrews in search of any resources that might explain why he died, what his death accomplished, and how he can be a priest when he is not descended from Levi. In Melchizedek, the author of Hebrews discovers a vital clue that provides exegetical leverage: there exists an eternal priesthood superior to the Levitical priesthood.

Hebrews quotes directly from the text of Genesis for the name of the king, his kingdom, and his vocation as "priest of the Most High God" but, for whatever reason, omits the presentation of bread and wine. A low-hanging Eucharistic fruit if there ever was one, the author leaves it for later Christian writers to pick. Instead, he summarizes the setting of Gen. 14:17-20—Abraham has just defeated the kings who had taken Lot captive—and focuses on the blessing given by Melchizedek and the tithe given by Abraham. (He does not quote the words of the blessing, which nonetheless resonate with other themes in Hebrews such as God as creator of heaven and earth [1:2, 10; 11:3] and the subjugation of enemies [1:13; 10:13]). Employing a rabbinic technique that argues from the silence of the text, in v. 3 the author notes the sudden appearance of Melchizedek and observes that Genesis offers no statement about his background and his abrupt departure makes no mention of his death. The remarkable conclusion he draws—that he has no beginning or end—is perhaps not self-evident to modern readers. It is in this sense that he resembles the Son of God, who was with God before creation and will remain at God's right hand forever (1:2, 6; 10:12).

If even Abraham gives him a tithe, the author explains further, then he must be someone extraordinary (7:4-10). Receiving a tithe is not exceptional, however, as the Levites do the same from their own brothers. It is not just the receiving of the tithe that makes Melchizedek special, but his ancestry. He and Abraham are not cut from the same cloth, and so this story is not simply one brother giving a tithe to another. The progenitor of the family of Israel tithes to someone who has no family at all. Turning from the question of his birth to his death, the author highlights a crucial difference between Melchizedek and the Levites, namely, they die but he lives. Because of his descent from Abraham, moreover, one could almost say that Levi was present for this exchange and thus clearly subordinate to Melchizedek. Hence, according to Hebrews, the argument for the superiority of Jesus's priesthood "according to the order of Melchizedek" is not a theological or sacerdotal innovation.

Lest one conclude that the story of Melchizedek is of purely antiquarian interest, the author spells out the implications for his readers (7:11-28). Although the focus here is on affairs as presented in the Bible, the discussion reflects some familiarity with debates in the Second Temple period (Horbury 1983). God never intended for the Levitical priesthood to be complete in itself or to last forever. God's speech in Ps. 110:4 appointing a priest to the order of Melchizedek is taken by the author of Hebrews as evidence that the Levitical priesthood did not bring perfection. If it had, there would be no need for God to appoint a priest to a different priesthood. This is no small matter because the author sees an intimate relationship between the priesthood and the law. A change in priesthood will mean that the people will interact with God's law in a different way. This includes Jesus's priesthood as well because he does not meet the normal qualifications stipulated in Torah. From the tribe of Judah, he has no familial right to serve at the altar, but his royal lineage qualifies him to receive the proclamation of Ps. 110:1-3 and, therefore, to be appointed to the order of Melchizedek. Yet even his birth into the tribe of Judah is not sufficient for this appointment since it is an eternal order. More than his birth, it is because of his death and "through the power of an indestructible life" (7:16) that he is the worthy recipient of God's call.

Jesus's unique qualifications, which include the establishment of his priesthood with a divine oath (7:20-22), make him fit to overcome the deficiencies of the Levitical priesthood of Aaron and become "the guarantor of a better covenant" (7:20-22). But it is important to note that Hebrews argues not that the earlier priesthood is evil or misguided, only that it was inadequate with respect to its efficacy and duration. The necessity of repeating the sin offerings on a regular basis implies that the "weak and ineffectual" system laid out in the Pentateuch was never intended to operate in perpetuity (Lev. 16:11-19; Num. 28:1-8; cf. Heb. 7:18; 9:6). The "holy, blameless, undefiled" sacrifice of Jesus the Son appointed as a priest by God's spoken oath, by contrast, was "once-for-all" (7:26-27). He is therefore singularly qualified to intercede on behalf of the people and enable them to draw near to God. By establishing a perfect and eternal priesthood outside the Levitical line and thus a different covenant relationship with God, Jesus has thereby inaugurated what Melchizedek foreshadowed.

The new covenant: Sin and the sacrifice of Jesus (8:1–10:18)

So that his audience will not get lost in the details of his argument, the author helpfully announces his "main point" in Heb. 8:1-6. *Kephalaion* can also mean "summary," an apt term for the way his remarks in v. 1 recapitulate the main theme of Hebrews 7. If earlier chapters have established the identity of and special role played by Jesus—the "who" and the "what"—Hebrews 8 turns to the "where." The author extends his analysis of the Levitical system from the priesthood itself to the setting in which Aaron and his successors carried out their priestly duties. His commentary pertains to the tabernacle in the wilderness, not to the temple in Jerusalem that falls to the Romans in 70 CE. He may nonetheless have expected his audience to make comparisons or discern parallels between contemporary cultic activity and liturgical practices of long ago.

Exodus contains detailed guidelines for the construction of the tabernacle the author of Hebrews has in mind when he mentions the sanctuary "that is a sketch [*hypodeigma*] and shadow [*skia*] of the heavenly one" (8:5; cf. Acts 7:44). According to Exod. 25:1–30:38, God gives instructions on everything from the dimensions of the tent, the contents of the ark of the covenant, and the materials used in fabricating the curtains to the ornamentation on the ephod worn by the priest, the placement of the furniture, and the recipe used in making the incense. Hebrews quotes God's command to Moses in Exod. 25:40 that he make everything "according to the pattern" that was shown to him on Sinai. Many scholars believe the author's use of this text occurs under the influence of a Platonic worldview (Thompson 1982). Hellenistic Jewish writers such as Philo of Alexandria as well as Christian writers like Origen draw on Platonic ideas to elucidate or allegorize biblical texts that, on their surface, might seem opaque or lend themselves to multiple interpretations. Plato conceived of the universe as existing on two levels: the material world, perceived through the senses and characterized by change and imperfection, and the world of "Forms," perceived by the mind and characterized by permanence and incorruptibility. Knowledge of the latter is true knowledge as its object is eternal, whereas the physical world exists only as a dim reflection or inferior copy of the Forms, which serve as a sort of blueprint for objects encountered in the realm of space, time, and matter (*Tim.* 28a).

It is natural to wonder if the relationship between the "pattern" (*typos*) consulted by Moses on Sinai and the earthly sanctuary built in the wilderness is understood by Hebrews in accordance with similarly dualistic metaphysical assumptions. Other passages seem to presuppose dichotomies (earthly/heavenly; visible/invisible; tangible/intangible) that are consistent with a Platonic worldview expressed most famously in the "allegory of the cave." God exists eternally in a realm that will not undergo alteration, unlike the mutable world he has created (Heb. 1:10-12). The "greater and perfect" tabernacle in which Jesus serves as high priest is one "not made with hands, that is, not of this creation" (9:11; if Jesus were on earth, according to 8:4, "he would not be a priest at all"). Ancient Israelite ritual involves "sketches [*hypodeigmata*] of the heavenly things" and is conducted in a "sanctuary made by human hands, a mere copy [*antitypos*] of the true one" (9:23-24). Not only do physical structures have this derivative character but the law, too, contains only a "shadow" (*skia*) but not the "true form" (*eikōn*) of "good things to come" (10:1). Faith likewise enables the believer to discern "things not seen" (11:1).

These antitheses are not unique to Plato, as many scholars have noted (Hurst 1990: 7–42). Apocalyptic texts such as 2 Baruch, 4 Ezra, and especially Revelation feature the motif of a heavenly prototype for the earthly temple and feature parallels between the worship offered above and below. Paul also reflects on the differences between the temporary and the eternal, though the "tent" he mentions may be the body and not the temple (2 Cor. 4:16–5:1). The eschatological nature of these parallel texts is a reminder of a key difference between Hebrews and Platonic idealism. Particular events in history play a minor role for the Greek philosophers. For Hebrews, however, history tells a story, set in specific times and places. This story—a true story, the author would hasten to add, with even more significance than its "characters" sometimes realize—has a beginning, a middle, and an end. The author is seeking to impress on his audience that their appearance comes at a point in this story that is not far from its climax "in these last days" (1:2). In one sense, the climax came already in the quite recent past at Calvary. The denouement will come with the return of Christ, participation in God's "rest," and the fulfillment of God's promises (4:1-11; 9:15; 10:35-39; 11:16, 39-40; 13:14). In this way, Hebrews turns Platonism "on its side," so to speak, so that the contrast between type and antitype is framed in terms of the past, on the one hand, and the present, on the other (Johnson 2006: 201–202). A "vertical" hierarchy is thus translated into a "horizontal" or temporal scheme in which the past is prologue to or foreshadowing of an auspicious present and (one hopes) a glorious future.

Few lines express this perspective on the author's thesis more succinctly than Heb. 8:6: "But Jesus has now obtained a more excellent ministry, and to that degree, his is the mediator of a better covenant, which has been enacted through better promises." The notion that a superior ministry has its corollary in a "better covenant" is a restatement of the principle that a change in priesthood entails a change in the law (7:12). God's promises are never far from sight in the exposition of Hebrews. Serendipitously, "promise" (*epangelia*) and "good news" (*euangelion*) differ by only a few letters. Thematically, for Hebrews, they are closely related as well. Without a grounding in God's promises, the gospel is bereft of content. "He who has promised" (10:23) is used as a circumlocution for God, whose promises to Abraham are mentioned on multiple occasions (6:13-15, 17; 7:6; 11:9, 11). These include allusions to the land he is to receive as well as progeny, against all odds ("the power of procreation"). Some promised blessings, however, have been held in reserve (11:13, 39; 10:36) so that the audience may be counted among those of Abraham's descendants who are heirs to the promises if they remain faithful (6:12). The promises that remain open to a future fulfillment include salvation (1:14; cf. 9:15: redemption from "transgressions") and "a kingdom that cannot be shaken" in heaven (12:26-28).

Covenants (*diathēkē*) are the vehicle for the delivery of God's promises (8:13; 9:1-4, 15-17, 20; 10:16, 27; 12:24; 13:20). Had the first covenant been "faultless," he reasons by way of a counterfactual, "there would have been no need to look for a second one" (8:7). As if to preempt the charge that Christian claims about Jesus imply that God is, at best, capricious or, at worst, unfaithful to promises made in the past beginning with Abraham, in Heb. 8:8-13 the author cites Jer. 31:31-34, the longest biblical quotation in the New Testament. From this text, the author seeks to demonstrate that God had intended to do something "new" all along. In v. 8, the plural pronoun "them" in the introductory formula ("God finds fault with them when he says") appears to refer to the Israelites who had forsaken the covenant, but it would not be wrong to infer a critique of the first covenant when one considers the language of "fault" in the preceding verse.

The text of Jeremiah largely conforms to the LXX version of an oracle originally delivered in the context of the Babylonian destruction of the temple in 586 BCE. It offers a ray of hope that is unusual in Jeremiah. "The days [that] are surely coming" are better days than those the residents of Jerusalem were enduring in Jeremiah's day. Hebrews appears to be drawn to his mention of a "new covenant." As rare as it is in the New Testament, "new covenant" language is even rarer in the Hebrew Bible. In fact, only Jer. 31:31-34 makes explicit use of it. Whether he is relying on a different LXX manuscript or introducing the change on his own, the author of Hebrews quotes Jer. 31:31 as saying that God will "complete" (*synteleso*) rather than "establish" (*diathēsomai*) this covenant. This alteration is potentially significant in that it suggests on the part of Hebrews an understanding that God is not discarding the covenant made with Abraham and affirmed through Moses and replacing it with an altogether different covenant but, rather, perfecting or bringing the first covenant to fulfillment. "Perfection" language in Hebrews from the same semantic range is consistent with this motif (Peterson 1982). Hebrews also follows the LXX text of Jeremiah when it departs from the Masoretic Text (MT) in v. 10. According to the MT, the failure of the Israelites to continue in the covenant occurs "though [the Lord] was their husband." The LXX has God respond to their infidelity with indifference ("so I had no concern for them"; it has been suggested that the LXX has translated a Hebrew text that substitutes *ga ʿal* ["ignore or abandon"] for *ba ʿal* ["husband"]; cf. Steyn 2011: 254).

Any flaw in the first covenant has to do with its inability to elicit from the people the desired response of obedience. What is new about the covenant inaugurated by Jesus is its interiority. Because its laws are written on their hearts, the people will have the capacity to keep it. The author exhorts his audience to exhort one another (3:12-13; 10:25), but "they shall not teach one another" when this covenant is fully established because of the intimacy of the relationship with God it makes possible. Given the identification of Jesus as mediator in Hebrews (8:6; 9:15; 12:24), it is somewhat surprising for the author to see the Jeremiah text as evidence of a more direct, less mediated means of access to the throne of grace. Jesus's solidarity with humans in their weakness likely helps to account for this seeming paradox.

The author's commentary on Jeremiah in Heb. 8:13 calls for some consideration of claims that this perspective constitutes a form of supersessionism, that is, the belief that God has rejected Israel and replaced it with the church. The author states that the establishment of a new covenant means that God has made the first one obsolete. It may be that "obsolete" (RSV; NIV; NRSV) conveys a harsher assessment of the first covenant than *pepalaiōken* merits, but to translate it as "made old" may be too weak, since anything "new" by definition means that something else becomes "old" in comparison. Hebrews does not suggest that God's covenant with Israel was a misguided enterprise from the outset. It does not distinguish belief in Christ from "the superstition of the Jews," as one finds in the preface of the second-century *Epistle to Diognetus*. Nor is there anything like what one finds in *Epistle of Barnabas*, another second-century text which says explicitly that the covenant belonging to the Jews is broken and that it is foolishness to believe that the new covenant is "both theirs and ours" (4.6-8). A supersessionist reading is further mitigated by the fact that Hebrews does not connect the failure of Israel to keep the covenant with a rejection of Jesus as Messiah, as the author's prooftext from Jeremiah depicts this failure as having commenced long before his first advent. Whether he is writing before or after the destruction of the temple by the Romans, the author is not engaging in a form of "theological *Schadenfreude*" (Svartvik 2011: 86). According to Hebrews, God's readiness to augment the first covenant at such a fundamental level nevertheless suggests that reliance on any covenant arrangements that have not undergone the renewal discovered in Jeremiah will not remain a viable modus vivendi indefinitely.

Hebrews is distinctive among early Jewish and Christian writers in terms of the degree to which the author stresses the "new" covenant, but the terminology can be found elsewhere, albeit without reference to the Jeremiah oracle (Lehne 1990: 32–61). The Qumran community sees itself as a "new covenant" separated from and more faithful than other Jewish groups (CD 6.19; 8.21; 19.13). Paul contrasts the new covenant of which he is a minister and whose members have hearts on which the Spirit of the living God has written with the "ministry of death, chiseled in letters on stone tablets" (2 Cor. 3:1-11). He may be thinking of Jeremiah, but he spends more time on the incident narrated in Exod. 34:29-35. Earlier, in 1 Cor. 11:25, he hands on a Last Supper tradition that has Jesus speak of "the new covenant in [his] blood." His language here most closely resembles Luke's account of the Last Supper (22:20). While Hebrews in a sense argues from the "solution" represented by Jesus's death as an atoning sacrifice for sin to the "problem" its author perceives in the first covenant, these texts raise the possibility that this notion and the attendant understanding of continuity and discontinuity in God's dealings with Israel may have been shared by Jesus himself.

Although the first covenant "will soon disappear," the author still has more to say about it (9:1-28). Rituals performed on the Day of Atonement and their underlying rationale are his primary focus in Hebrews 9–10. He states that he cannot go into great detail but includes just enough particulars concerning "regulations for worship" (*dikaiōmata latreias*) to establish his credibility as a reliable interpreter of the institutions of that covenant that are described in various sections of the Pentateuch (9:5; cf. Lev. 16:20-28; Num. 19:1-10). Mention of the ark of the covenant and its contents—Aaron's rod, the tablets of the law, and a golden urn containing manna—provide a reminder of God's miraculous provision for the Israelites who strayed from the first covenant as well as the stone tablets on which the law was engraved, in contrast to the new covenant written on the heart described by Jeremiah.

Of special interest to the author is the manner in which sacrifices performed in the tabernacle on the Day of Atonement reveal their provisional character. Repetition per se is not an indicator of ontological inferiority, but the singularity of Jesus's sacrifice carries more theological weight here than it does in any other early Christian text (Moore 2015:166–88). That priests must "continually" offer sacrifices nonetheless repeats a motif from Heb. 7:27 that the author treats as a sign of the relative inefficacy of their offerings, whether they are made for willful or unintentional sins (9:6-7). These priestly duties are, according to Heb. 9:8, a "symbol" or "parable" (*parabolē*) of or for "the present time." All such earthly events occurring "until the time comes to set things right" (*kairou diorthōseōs*) thus have a provisional character inasmuch as none of them can "perfect the conscience" (9:9-10). Jesus's own sacrifice alone accomplishes this purification of the conscience, that is, the internal rather than the external (9:11-14). He can do this because, as "high priest of the good things that have come, . . . through the greater and more perfect tent" he has entered the heavenly sanctuary once for all to obtain eternal redemption. Moreover, this sacrifice is "without blemish" because Jesus is without sin. For Hebrews, then, the setting for the sacrifice as well as the offering itself are superior to the offerings made in the Holy of Holies under the first covenant. Such an argument would have special poignancy if, as one scholar has suggested, Hebrews was written as a synagogue homily to be delivered on *Tisha be-Av*, the date on which both the first and second temples were destroyed (Gelardini 2005).

There is some confusion when it comes to the next stage of the argument for Jesus's superiority as a mediator (9:15-22). *Diathēkē* can mean both a "covenant" in the biblical sense and also "will" or "testament" in the legal sense current in Greek and Roman jurisprudence. Translators regularly switch back and forth between these different senses in the short space of vv. 15-17, despite their distinct meanings and even though every other occurrence in Hebrews—more than a dozen—is always rendered "covenant." (A similar polyvalence is found in Gal. 3:15-17.) Most translations, like the NRSV, render *diathēkē* as "will" in vv. 16-17: "Where a will is involved, the death of the one who made it must be established. For a will takes effect only at death, since it is not in force as long as the one who made it is alive." In v. 18, most translators resume their use of "covenant," despite the organic flow of the author's argument ("Hence not even the first *diathēkē* was inaugurated without blood").

Is the author engaging in bilingual wordplay? Is it possible that he is unaware of the confusion he has created? Or is there some way to make sense of his usage in its literary and theological context? It has been suggested that rendering *diathēkē* consistently as "covenant" fits with ancient Israelite practice (Hahn 2005: 80–88). Parties to a covenant invoke a curse of death on anyone found to be in violation, as one sees in Exodus 32 and at other points in the Pentateuch narratives. Animals slain as part of the covenant ritual represent that curse on those who break the covenant. Hebrews draws out the legal implications of the liturgy that accompanied the establishment of the first covenant. The author is speaking specifically of the Sinai covenant and the curse of death attached to it and is explaining why a death is required. To paraphrase Heb. 9:16-17, the death of the unfaithful party must be borne when the covenant is broken, and by definition, the terms of this particular covenant have not gone into effect when that party is still living. The terms of that covenant are not abrogated. Jesus bears that curse and thus fulfills its terms.

To underline this point about the purpose of both covenants and the mechanism for their fulfillment, the author states that "without the shedding of blood there is no forgiveness of sins" (9:22). This motif appears in the Jeremiah oracle and will reappear at the end of Hebrews 9 when the author says that Christ was "offered once to bear the sins of many" (9:28). The summary of the priestly activities in the tabernacle also cites Exod. 24:8 where Moses sprinkles the scrolls, the people, and the vessels for worship with blood. Whereas the MT and the LXX both read, "Behold, the blood of the covenant," Hebrews reads, "This [*touto*] is the blood of the covenant," as do the words of institution in the Synoptic accounts of the Last Supper which likewise highlight the purpose of Jesus's shed blood "for the forgiveness of sins" (Mt. 26:27-28). Hebrews never alludes to the Last Supper, and so this slight alteration of Exod. 24:8 may have occurred under the influence of Eucharistic language used in the early church rather than as a result of the author having read one of the Synoptic Gospels.

Jesus's appearance "at the end of the age" is to remove sin (9:26). Postmortem judgment awaits all humans in the absence of any such efficacious sacrifice. A second appearance will be for the completion of his work, "not to deal with sin, but to save those who are eagerly awaiting him" (9:28). This formulation is informed by the custom on the Day of Atonement, when the people would wait expectantly for the high priest to emerge from the Holy of Holies, thereby confirming that God had accepted his sacrifice for their sins (Lane 1991: 250–51; according to *b.Yoma* 39b, a red strip of cloth tied to the horn of the scapegoat in the Yom Kippur ritual would turn white to indicate that it had been accepted). The "already" of Jesus's death and all it accomplished is to be followed by the "not yet" of the Second Coming. This glorious arrival will presumably coincide with the arrival of the faithful at the "heavenly Jerusalem" (12:22).

The central expository section concludes in Heb. 10:1-18 with a consideration of Christ's once-for-all (*ephapax*: 7:27; 9:12; 10:10) sacrifice and its superiority to the animal sacrifices offered year after year. This stage of the exposition takes the form of one more a fortiori argument, coming after comparisons of Jesus's ministry with the Levitical priesthood (7:1-28), the first covenant it was intended to serve (8:1-13), and the sanctuary in which its rituals were conducted (9:1-28). The author proceeds in vv. 1-4 on the basis of textual premises that he expects his audience to accept. One sees the same rhetorical strategy at work when he cites the scriptural testimony of another "day" as evidence that Joshua's leadership had not culminated in a final "rest" for the people and the reference in Jeremiah to the need for a second covenant as an admission of inadequacy in the first one (4:8; 8:7). From the sheer fact that the sacrifices of the Levitical system are still offered on an annual basis, the author reasons that they must not have fully accomplished their purpose: "Otherwise, would they not have ceased being offered?" Personal experience validates his argument insofar as worshippers retain a consciousness (*syneidēsis*) of sin. A conscience "purif[ied] from dead works" facilitates "worship [of] the living God" (9:14). In fact, he claims, the repetition of the sacrifice promotes "a reminder of sin" even if the larger aim was to provide for atonement.

This inability to accomplish its aims leads the author to characterize the law as containing "only a shadow of the good things to come and not the true form of these realities" (10:1; Col. 2:17 speaks similarly of various rites as "only a shadow of what is to come"). He has already spoken of "the good things that have [already] come" in reference to Jesus's once-for-all sacrifice (9:11). Here he speaks from the temporal perspective of the priests and worshippers under the first covenant. The "good things" still to come would thus include Jesus's death and the sanctification and forgiveness it makes possible. It also includes the parousia of Christ to which he refers a few verses earlier as well as the eschatological "rest" they will enjoy with the "assembly of the firstborn" in the heavenly Jerusalem (4:1-10; 12:22-24).

For purifying the conscience, much less for the removal of sin itself, the blood of goats is insufficient (10:4). The crucial difference between the offering of Christ and that of goats and bulls is not simply that the former is singular and the latter is repeated. It is that animals do not willingly submit and therefore cannot be perfect in the way that Jesus is (Moore 2015: 174–75). To make this point in Heb. 10:5-10, the author puts Ps. 40:6-8 on the lips of Jesus "when he came into the world," citing it in a form that closely matches the LXX version (Steyn 2011: 282–97). This formula is reminiscent of the incarnational language found in the Gospel of John (e.g., 1:9; 3:19; 12:46; 16:21, 28), which complements the accent on the preexistence of the Son in the exordium of Heb. 1:3. One might also construe the author's incorporation of the citation as an instance of "quoting" the earthly Jesus in the act of quoting Scripture as a reference to himself and in which he in turn quotes himself ("Then I said, 'See, God, I have come to do your will'").

Where the MT has the psalmist say that God has "dug ears" so that he can hear and obey rather than attempting to make satisfaction through sacrifices, the LXX, followed by Hebrews, says that God has prepared a "body." Given the association of hearing with obedience and the emphasis in Hebrews on doing God's will, the MT would have fit the author's purposes. But the substitution of "body" for "ears" additionally accords with Jesus's suffering of death in the body that he endures when he takes on flesh and blood (2:14-17; 5:7-10). Hebrews departs from the LXX slightly when it says that God "took no pleasure" in burnt offerings: instead of that he has "requested" no such offerings. God had, in fact, instituted that system, after all, and the Israelites were therefore obligated to observe its ordinances. That the very system God had established would fail to please him suggests to the author that it was never meant to be an end in itself but, rather, was all along intended as a temporary arrangement put in place until something "better" (kreittōn; cf. 9:23) should replace or supplement it. In Heb. 10:8-10, the author does not condemn the sacrificial system described in the Hebrew Bible, even if Jesus's fulfillment of its requirements now renders further blood offerings superfluous.

By slightly altering the syntax of the LXX, the author also has Jesus express his sense of mission more forcefully (Mitchell 2007: 201). Both the MT and the LXX find his advent foretold "in the book." But where the former has the speaker "delighting" in and the latter "intending" to do God's will, Hebrews has Jesus declare it as his explicit and unequivocal purpose to do God's will. Not only is the performance of the divine will the very reason for his coming, as the author reiterates in v. 9, but it is also foretold in Scripture. Jesus voluntarily subordinates his will to God's when he offers himself as a propitiation for sin. Sanctification takes place "by that will" (v. 10). It is unclear whether this will belong to God or to Jesus, but in Hebrews, the two have merged to such a degree that a distinction is hardly imaginable. The notion that God prefers obedience to burnt offerings is expressed so often in the Bible that it can sound like a truism (1 Sam. 15:22; Ps. 51:18-19; Isa. 1:11-15; Amos 5:21-24). For Hebrews, it is important that Jesus satisfies this requirement and makes it possible for others to do likewise.

To borrow a term from the stage, a final element of this extended comparison has to do with "blocking" (10:11-18). Priests under the first covenant must stand day after day as they make their offerings "again and again." Described this way, their ministry sounds, quite literally, exhausting. This image of priests standing perpetually at attention is juxtaposed with that of Christ seated at God's right hand, where he is waiting until his "enemies" are made "a footstool for his feet" (vv. 12-13). His work completed, he is now ensconced in heaven, above the angels. This allusion to the enthronement psalm (110:1) recycles the same citation found in Heb. 1:3, 13, and weds the role of the Son with that of the high priest. Another re-citation—of Jer. 31:33-34, excerpted and paraphrased—provides the closing bracket of the exposition that began in Hebrews 8. The excerpt includes God's promise to write his laws on the people's hearts and minds and to "remember their sins and their lawless deeds no more," a fitting conclusion to his argument that Jesus's ministry does away with "reminder[s] of sin" (10:3) and that his obedience has the power to transform their recalcitrant wills.

By faith: Drawing near to God and to one another (10:19–11:40)

It is now possible to "enter the sanctuary by the blood of Jesus" (10:19-25). Going "by the new and living way that he opened for us . . . through his flesh," however, requires confidence (*parrēsia*). A guilty conscience inhibits true worship of God. The author again exhorts the audience to "approach with a true heart in full assurance, with our hearts sprinkled clean . . . and bodies washed with pure water." These reminders of their conversion are meant to help them weather any "wavering" and "hold fast to the confession."

Absenteeism from their common assemblies is a sign that their initial enthusiasm is waning (v. 25). Time spent together is especially important for the solidarity of a group understanding itself as a household (3:1-6; 10:21), as social bonds and belief structures are mutually reinforcing. It is furthermore difficult to "provoke one another to love and good works" and provide encouragement unless they are physically present in the same location, yet it is all the more imperative "as [they] see the Day approaching" (v. 25). The earliest non-Christian descriptions of Christian groups—the correspondence between Trajan and Pliny—mention their communal gatherings. This information is gleaned by imperial authorities who had interrogated members to determine if they were subversive elements in Roman society. Whether it is fear of such harassment, shame in the face of stigma or ostracism, a sense of intellectual pride, or an interest in other cults with a presence in the city, they must not neglect to meet together "as is the habit of some" (deSilva 2000: 341–43). Jewish sources indicate that regular attendance was not a peculiarly Christian concern and that withdrawal from fellowship was viewed as a symptom or a cause of spiritual disaffection.

Apostasy is the most alarming form of alienation from the perspective of insiders who "hold fast to the confession" (10:26-31). The author has just exhorted them to remain confident but now evokes the opposite emotion of fear in the starkest of terms. "Willful persistence in sin" is tantamount to "falling away," and the consequences include "a fearful prospect of judgment, and a fury of fire" (vv. 26-27; cf. 6:4-6). "Receiving knowledge of the truth" means that they may not plead ignorance as to the requirements of their faith, even if it was not possible to grasp its full meaning prior to their conversion. If violators of the law of Moses die without mercy, then those who have "spurned the Son of God, profaned the blood of the covenant by which they were sanctified, and outraged the Spirit of grace" face an even more calamitous fate (v. 29). "Spurning" (*katapatēsas*) is, more literally, "trampling," a gesture of disdain required in the persecution of Japanese Christians in the seventeenth century who were forced to tread upon images of Jesus under threat of torture. "It is a fearful thing to fall into the hands of the living God" who will, in a turn of poetic justice, make Jesus's enemies— those who would trample on him—into his footstool (v. 31; cf. 1:13: 10:13).

The immediate specter of persecution has some members wondering if the distant prospect of divine vengeance is nonetheless worth the risk (10:32-39). To steer them away from such a ruinous course, the author seeks to rekindle the warm feelings "of those earlier days" following their conversion. He reminds them that they "cheerfully accepted the plundering of [their] possessions" as part of the abuse they endured and commends them for recognizing that they "possessed something better and more lasting" (v. 34). Their confidence in this "possession" is something that they must not "throw away" (*mē apobalēte*) or else they will forfeit "what was promised" (v. 36). This "possession" metaphor extends to the end of Hebrews 10. Those who remain faithful in the face of persecution, according to most translations of v. 39, will be "saved." *Peripoiēsis* often refers to property or possessions (Eph. 1:14; 1 Pet. 2:9) and therefore it would be more literal to say that the faithful will "possess their souls" (Vulg.: *adquisitio animae*).

A composite quotation from Isa. 26:20 and Hab. 2:3-4 LXX reinforces the author's call for endurance in Heb. 10:37-39. Hebrews understands "the one who is coming" in Isaiah to be Jesus. That he "will not delay" adds a note of eschatological urgency as well as comfort to Hebrews's beleaguered readers. The text of Habakkuk has a complicated history, and Hab. 2:4b is quoted by Paul in other contexts (Rom. 1:17; Gal. 3:11; cf. Attridge 1989: 301–304). It is often translated as "the just/righteous [one(s)] shall live by faith." Who is "the just/righteous one," and by whose faith will the just/righteous live? When the author of Hebrews quotes it, is he applying it to the audience and any person with faith, or does he have in mind a particular righteous person? And does the faith of which he speaks belong to the individual or should it be understood as the fidelity of God or of Jesus? By inverting the order of the clauses in the LXX, Hebrews makes "my righteous one" instead of "the coming one" the subject of both clauses in v. 38. To shrink back now would be very poor timing indeed. What does it look like to "live by faith"? The author provides an answer in the following chapter.

The author helpfully supplies a definition of *pistis* at the outset of Hebrews 11: "Now faith is the assurance of things hoped for, the conviction of things not seen." However much its terminology (*hypostasis; elenchus*) is used in philosophical and theological discourse, this is not intended as an exhaustive or technical definition covering every aspect of faith. It is the opening statement in an encomium with a special emphasis on faith's function in relating the visible to the invisible. "Living by the Unseen" is how Clarence Jordan renders the anaphoric *en pistei* in his "Cotton Patch" translation into colloquial Southern English. Anaphora is the rhetorical technique of repeating a word or phrase at the beginning of successive statements for rhetorical effect. The author of Hebrews repeats "by faith" over and over to create the impression that the cited examples are representative of a larger group and to invite his audience to join in the procession that stretches across time.

With his thesis clearly announced, the author embarks on a survey of ancient Jewish history (11:4-38). Example lists and selective historical summaries are often used by Hellenistic Jewish and early Christian writers to provide moral instruction or theological interpretation of past events (Cosby 1988). Such lists are found in Sirach 44–50, 1 Macc. 2:51-60, Acts 7, and 1 Clem. 9.2–12.8, as well as in Greco-Roman writers like Isocrates, Cicero, and Plutarch. Especially when carried out with rhetorical sophistication, the accumulation of examples has a persuasive force that operates differently from the tightly constructed exegetical arguments found elsewhere in Hebrews. The selection of representatives from that history is based on the faith he perceives them to have demonstrated. Each figure named in this "roll call" of the faithful reveals an aspect of the author's understanding of faith and yields a lesson that he wants to impart to his audience.

Abel is the first of three antediluvian figures to be introduced, if only because, chronologically, no other candidates for inclusion seem appropriate at the head of the list (vv. 4-7). His reputation for righteousness is attested in biblical and non-biblical sources (1 En. 22.7; Mt. 23:35; 1 Jn 3:12). Faith is not attributed to him in Genesis, but it is perhaps in the principle that "the righteous shall live by faith" that the author finds a warrant for his characterization. "Better" and "living" sacrifices are also pervasive themes in Hebrews (cf. 9:23; 10:11-14, 19-20). Enoch's time on the biblical stage is even briefer than Abel's. The enigmatic reference in Gen. 5:24 to Enoch walking with and then being taken by God gave rise to a body of speculative literature in the Second Temple period. The author regards the mere fact of his belief in God's existence as exceptional in the depraved generations leading up to the flood. It seems self-evident that "whoever would approach him must believe that he exists" (11:6). First-century writers like Plutarch, however, sometimes preferred atheism if the alternative was a superstitious religiosity that breeds craven fear of the deity. Noah exercises prudent caution when warned by God "about events as yet unseen," a posture described in the same language as Jesus's own "godly fear" (*eulabeia* [5:7]).

Abraham receives more attention than any other figure in Hebrews 11 (vv. 8-12, 17-19). Faith equips him to set out when called to leave his land and his people without any clear vision of where he is going. More daunting still, in Gen. 12:4-9 when he goes to the land of Canaan which he had been promised, he finds that it is already occupied—by Canaanites, naturally. Still trusting that it is part of his inheritance, he sojourns there "as in a foreign land," dwelling in tents, the precariousness of which contrasts with the "city that has foundations, whose architect and builder is God" (Heb. 11:9-10). Descendants "as many as the stars of heaven" constitute the other part of his inheritance. Childlessness and old age threaten this promise, which is nevertheless fulfilled through faith. Whose faith facilitates the miraculous birth of offspring is textually and grammatically unclear: Is Abraham or Sarah the subject of v. 11? Commentators are divided on the question (Greenlee 1990). Both have moments when they seem less than fully certain that God's promises will come to fruition (Gen. 12:11-13; 17:17-18; 18:9-15), but the relative insignificance of Abraham's first son, Ishmael, suggests that Sarah is a key player in the drama of faith alongside her husband in giving birth to Isaac. Had she known of it, her consternation at the offering of Isaac would surely have been great. Abraham faces this test alone and passes it by faith (vv. 17-20; cf. Gen. 22:1-8). It is simultaneously the most celebrated yet most disturbing story from the Abraham cycle. Many early Christian writers read it typologically in connection with the sacrifice of Jesus, though that connection is not emphasized as heavily or as explicitly in Hebrews as one might expect (Swetnam 1981). The content of Abraham's faith includes his belief that God "is able even to raise someone from the dead," and this enables him to perform a deed that most parents would likely find to be equally impossible. He receives Isaac back "figuratively speaking" (*en parabolē*) in that, literally speaking, he never completes the sacrificial act (v. 19).

Inserted in the middle of the Abraham material is a preliminary summary that clarifies what the various exemplars have in common (vv. 13-16). At the end of Hebrews 11, the author will return to the point that they are all still waiting on God to fulfill promises made in the past and are furthermore aware that God has more in store for them than anything they may possess here and now. Their longing for a homeland is taken as evidence that it must exist somewhere, in heaven if not on earth. A homeland is normally a place from which one hails and to which one returns. In the case of the Israelites who leave Egypt, their desire to return to Egypt when the prospect of starvation arises is a troubling, if natural, response. Canaan, however, is not ultimately the homeland of those who sojourn "by faith." Their embrace of their status as "strangers and foreigners" is a lesson for the audience members who may be weighting the costs this status imposes, such as social stigma and forfeited civic rights (cf. Phil. 3:20; 1 Pet. 2:11; Koester 2001: 489). Faith makes it possible to be in the world but not of it while awaiting God's fulfillment of promises.

The march of exemplars resumes with Isaac, Jacob, and Joseph (vv. 20-22). Isaac's faith is oriented toward "things to come," coloring it with an element of hope even as he unwittingly blesses his younger son. Jacob's faith is seen in his blessing of Joseph's sons Ephraim and Manasseh, whereas Joseph's faith inspires a prediction of the exodus along with instructions to carry his bones to the land he was confident his descendants would one day possess. Uniting these patriarchs is an ability to see "from afar" (11:1, 3) the hoped-for fulfillment of God's promises, especially in the shadow of death (Bulley 1996: 414–18).

Moses receives extended treatment in vv. 23-28, where the emphasis falls on his defiance of human authorities. Initially, however, his parents are praised for this courageous faith. Although baby Moses is the grammatical subject of v. 23, it is Amram and Jochabed who, undaunted by the pharaoh's decree, hide their child for three months. In vv. 24-26, the adult Moses foregoes the privileges he enjoyed as the adoptive son of the pharaoh's daughter, "choosing rather to share ill-treatment with the people of God than to enjoy the fleeting pleasures of sin." He thus sets an example for the audience whom the author has commended for their solidarity with the persecuted and imprisoned in Heb. 10: 32-34. His preternatural vision enables him to consider "abuse suffered for the Christ to be greater wealth than the treasures of Egypt." Just as the renunciation of his status was a function of his discernment of his true family, the audience will have to learn about the rights and also the responsibilities of membership in God's house. It would be a sin of omission rather than commission, but to take the path of least resistance would nonetheless count as a failure of faith in the author's eyes to the extent that it represents a mistaken idea of where one's true inheritance lies. Understandably, Hebrews passes lightly over the circumstances that compel Moses to leave Egypt, though some manuscripts contain an extra sentence after v. 23 explaining that "by faith" Moses "killed the Egyptian because he observed the humiliation of his brothers." (Augustine [*Faust.* 22.70] and other ancient interpreters sometimes find fault with Moses for this "murder by faith.") Unlike the Exodus narrative as well as noncanonical versions of the story, Hebrews accentuates the manner in which Moses's faith translates into fearlessness. He is able to persevere through difficult times because "he saw him who is invisible."

After the treatment of Moses, the author accelerates his survey (vv. 29-31). Several examples appear in rapid succession, including that of the people passing through the Red Sea. Subsequent examples are drawn from the time of the conquest, from among the "winners" (those who encircled Jericho) and the "losers" (Rahab, a Gentile, who was spared the fate of her unbelieving neighbors because she acknowledged the God of the invading Israelites as the true God and acted accordingly). It is perhaps no accident that the survey bypasses the wilderness generation, as the period between their departure from Egypt and their entry into the Promised Land was not their finest hour in the author's view. Neither Aaron nor Joshua appears on the list here, despite their prominent roles in the desert wanderings. Their earlier appearances in Hebrews (4:8; 5:4; 7:11) mention the well-known parts they play in Israel's history but underscore their shortcomings.

A rhetorical question—"And what more should I say?"—signals that the catalogue is coming to an end (vv. 32-38). Orators employ such questions to leave the impression that many more examples might be listed if only time permitted. John Chrysostom knows the techniques of a master orator when he sees them and points out where the author breaks off his detailed list "lest he should be thought tedious" (*Hom. Heb.* 27.4). Name-dropping in such an allusive manner also presupposes a familiarity with these stories on the part of his audience. Commentators wonder about his choices from later Israelite history in v. 32, especially Jephthah, who is remembered for the rash vow that cost his daughter her life, and Samson, whose impulse control left something to be desired. David and Samuel are more obvious choices, yet their cameos here highlight what the list largely downplays. Kings, priests, and judges are not the stars of the show, and celebrated events such as the establishment of the monarchy at Jerusalem and the building of the temple go unmentioned (Eisenbaum 1997: 175–76). Prophets and martyrs enjoy higher status. The litany of examples to which the author alludes in his peroration includes many figures whose identity can be guessed, such as the women whose sons are raised by Elijah and Elisha (1 Kgs 17:17-24; 2 Kgs 4:18-37), Daniel in the lion's den, and the martyrs in 2 Maccabees. Other descriptions seem to apply to any number of figures. Through faith, they accomplished great feats (vv. 33-35a), but the author decides to end on a seemingly morbid note. Torture, mocking, floggings, imprisonment, stonings, even being sawn in two—their rejection by "the world" says more about them than the world realizes. It is the world that was unworthy of them, not vice versa (v. 38). Their alienation from the world is a badge of honor when viewed through the eyes of faith.

Whatever hardships the audience may be facing, this is a point he wants to impress on them. Not all those who wander are lost. It has not yet come to the point where they are roaming the deserts and mountains or hiding in caves, but there may come a time when they must leave the city and suffer (13:13-14). The author puts his audience into the larger story of God's people, which will not be complete until they all receive "what was promised" together (11:39-40).

It is often observed that Hebrews focuses more on the character of faith than on its precise object and that Jesus is presented as an example for the readers to follow like the other figures presented in Hebrews 11. Yet *pistis* in Hebrews is not a vague "faithfulness" that is entirely devoid of content. Jesus is more than an ethical model to emulate. He can be the object as well as the subject of faith. Believers are obligated to obey Jesus, according to Heb. 5:8-9, on account of his own obedience to God. As the Son relates to the Father, so Christians relate to the Son (Hamm 1990: 282). He is qualitatively different from the others who live "by faith" and not distinguished simply by the degree of faithfulness he exhibits. Without an implicit conviction that Jesus is somehow fundamentally different from others who might offer a similarly praiseworthy example of faith, even to the point of death, it is hard to see how his suffering and death can be efficacious in the way Hebrews describes. Were Jesus not who he is according to Hebrews, his death would be tragic but of no vicarious benefit.

Training for the kingdom of God (12:1-29)

The encomium to faith is not quite finished when Hebrews 11 ends and Hebrews 12 begins. There is one more person to whom the author directs their attention: Jesus, "the pioneer and perfecter" of the faithful (12:2). The author compares the life of faith to a race, and his lyrical description emphasizes the quality of endurance, the very quality his audience needs to embody in their current circumstances.

Author and audience alike take on the role of athlete in the race metaphor (12:1-4). As they compete, they are surrounded by a "cloud of witnesses." *Martys* can refer to an observer or, as one sees more commonly in subsequent centuries, to a particular kind of "witness" that takes the form of a faithful life laid down for a greater cause. Here it seems to function in both ways. These witnesses bear witness through the stories that elicited God's approval (11:2, 39) even as they watch the ongoing race as if assembled in a stadium where the runners are competing. This "cloud"—a crowd of spectators, really, who were once participants themselves—consists of Abel, Abraham, Jacob, Moses, Rahab, and the rest of the faithful lauded in the preceding chapter. That they have a stake in the results of the race is indicated by the author's remark that they "did not receive what was promised [cf. 11:13], since God had provided something better so that they would not, apart from us [i.e., the author and audience], be made perfect" (11:40). According to the logic of Heb. 11:39–12:2, if the audience drops the baton before reaching the finish line, then in some sense, everyone loses. With this rhetorical move, the author not only heightens the drama but also seeks to hold his readers to account for their decisions and stresses the role they play in the drama of salvation.

In order to finish the race that remains (*prokeimenon*), they must set their sights on that most faithful runner, Jesus. To make his point, the author employs the visually evocative devices of Greco-Roman orators such as *enargeia* and *phantasia*, rhetorical figures involving the use of vivid language to aid an audience in forming a mental image (Mackie 2017: 476–97). Their race will require endurance. As the "pioneer," Jesus has already run the race "for the sake of the joy that was set before (*prokeimeneis)* him" (12:2). Jesus was running toward a goal then, just as the audience ought to be now. He endured the cross and its shame because on the other side lay the joy of sitting at God's right hand over God's people. If they likewise endure, they will be able to join "the assembly of the firstborn" in the heavenly Jerusalem (12:22-23; perhaps it is no coincidence that *archēgos*, "pioneer," can mean a trailblazer as well as a city founder).

The race metaphor introduces the theme of endurance, which allows the author to address the topic of suffering now from a broadly theological rather than narrowly Christological perspective. They have had to endure abuse since their conversion but not yet martyrdom (12:4). By adding "yet," the author acknowledges that their trouble may not be over. Proverbs 3:11-12 supplies encouragement in Heb. 12:5-6, spoken not by Solomon to an unknown son in the distant past, but by God to this audience in the present. My son, God says, do not despise the discipline of the Lord, nor faint—*ekluō*, exactly what he says to avoid during their "race" in v. 3—when reproved by him. What you are experiencing, the author explains, is God's discipline (*paideia*; cognate terms occur eight times in this passage). They should not regard it as animosity or neglect. Rather, God is bringing it upon them precisely because they are God's children and need their heavenly father's love. This is how fatherhood and sonship work; the relationship entails discipline. It may not be pleasant, but it springs from well-meaning motivation and intends a positive outcome. If this is true with fallible human fathers who may not always know best, how much more is it true with God who knows all and can bring about not just maturity but the godly qualities of holiness, peace, and righteousness (12:9-10).

The author offers this reflection on the recontextualized proverb as a powerful encouragement to the readers. Their discipline is educative in nature rather than punitive or retributive. God is not the proximate cause of their suffering, nor is their sin mentioned as the reason God is allowing them to suffer (Croy 1998: 196–200). The vocative "my son" in Heb. 12:5 (=Prov. 3:11) takes on a deeper significance in light of the connection between Jesus's sonship and that of the readers. If Scripture identifies them as God's children, then they must remember that the testimony of Scripture reinterprets their experience in this instance. To wish for anything different is tantamount to forfeiting one's status as son and heir. Bastards (v. 8: *nothoi*) were exempt from the discipline of the *paterfamilias* in the Roman world, but they were also left out of the father's will. The author thus urges his readers to accept their hardships as a necessary part of their inheritance as God's legitimate children. For modern readers, the challenge is that this message could devolve into a picture of a sadistic, abusive father who delights in the whipping of his children. The author's comparison with human fathers works against this reading. Like good human fathers, the author suggests, God allows difficult experiences that will enable the children to grow into the very qualities they require. Were they not to become holy, peaceful, and righteous, they might have temporary pleasure but would remain apart from God's glorious presence for the long term.

Esau makes a rare New Testament appearance in Heb. 12:16-17 as a negative example of how one might respond to such paternal discipline. The author describes him as "immoral and godless," yet the only information he gives is that he disregarded his standing as a firstborn son in selling his birthright (*prōtotokia*), treating it as less important than a single meal. To value physical security over the birthright reflects misplaced priorities and a wavering faith from which the author seeks to dissuade his audience. When he wanted to inherit the blessing of the firstborn, he was rejected. Even though he sought it with tears, the decision could not be undone. The author makes no dogmatic statement about this episode. Merely hinting at the possibility is a chilling reminder of the warnings about repentance and apostasy in Heb. 6:4-6: to disdain one's place in God's household is to risk rejection even if the blessing is sought with tearful repentance.

With this warning still hanging in the air, in Heb. 12:18-29 the author returns to the generation of Israelites who wandered in the wilderness (cf. 3:7-4:11) and collapses separate episodes taking place in the Pentateuch at Sinai into a unified yet complex scene (Exod. 19:16-19; 20:18-19; Deut. 4:11-12, 24, 33; 5:23-26). Whereas the wilderness generation arrived at Sinai, the present readers have come to Mount Zion. The former evokes wonder and terror while the latter is still more awe-inspiring. The scene at Mount Zion in vv. 22-24 is a crowded one which overwhelms the reader. In arriving at "the city of God, the heavenly Jerusalem," they have come

> to innumerable angels in festal gathering, and to the assembly of the firstborn enrolled in heaven, and to God the judge of all, and to the spirits of the righteous made perfect, and to Jesus, the mediator of a new covenant, and to the sprinkled blood that speaks a better word than the blood of Abel. (Heb. 12:22c-24)

While the tone is decidedly more festive than what we have for the scene at Sinai, the presence of the divine judge in v. 23 nonetheless tempers the celebratory mood. Zion was identified as the site of God's future judgment according to Jewish apocalyptic traditions contemporaneous with Hebrews (4 Ezra 13:35-39). By allowing this undercurrent to come to the surface at this juncture, the author reminds the readers how much more fearful it will be for them if they now "refuse him who is speaking" (12:25). Now that they have come to Zion, the consequences of falling away for those who have been privileged with God's definitive revelation will be even more dreadful than the fate of those who turned away at Sinai (Koester 2001: 549–51)

The faithful will not be kept at a distance but, rather, will be granted the blessing of joining "the assembly of the firstborn" (v. 23). God is still "judge of all," but the spirits of the righteous have been made "perfect." They owe their "perfection" to Jesus, who is also in attendance as the living mediator of the covenant that brings complete and eternal forgiveness. It is in this sense that his "sprinkled blood . . . speaks a better word" than Abel, whose blood cried out for justice but not mercy (*Jub.* 4:3; *T. Benj.* 7:3-5).

Although they have approached this mountain at the end of their sojourn, the author still has concerns for their conduct there (vv. 25-29). The author again employs a fortiori reasoning: As the wilderness generation resisted the one who warned them, how could this community possibly escape if they resist the one now speaking from heaven? Is God the Father the one speaking here, as he has done much of the speaking throughout Hebrews? Or is it

Jesus since his blood was "speaking" in the previous verse? Was it the divine voice who issued warnings from Mount Sinai, or the voice of Moses ("the one who warned them on earth"), with whom the author has compared Jesus in Heb. 3:1-6? However one answers these questions, it is clear that the stakes are now higher than ever before. As Mount Sinai trembled, so too does God promise to make the very heavens quake (quoting Hag. 2:6). Moreover, this time the shaking of the earth will leave only those things that cannot be shaken. Some interpreters see this as a removal of all creation, the things which have been made, but others maintain that creation could be part of that which remains (Cockerill 2012: 664–72). The author and his readers are coming into possession of this kingdom that cannot be shaken, and therefore it is fitting that they render "acceptable worship," described in the same terms as the "reverence" (*eulabeia*) of Jesus the son whose prayers are heard by his heavenly father in Heb. 5:7. God is a "consuming fire" who will consume their sacrifices offered in reverence, just as he did those offered by the priests under the old covenant.

The author's belief that they were living in the last days (1:2) accounts for the urgency of his exhortation. In this regard, their situation parallels that of Noah, who was likewise warned (11:7: *chrēmatistheis*; cf. 12:25: *chrēmatizonta*) by God about an impending disruption on a global scale (cf. Gen. 6:5-8; Josephus, *Ant.* 1:75-76). Their "reverence and awe" demonstrate their awareness of living on a threshold, at a point where the old is vanishing and the new is coming into view (cf. Heb. 8:13). They are on the verge of entering the promised rest, as were the Israelites when they faltered in disobedience and failed to enter (3:7–4:11). For this reason, the citation in v. 29 of Deut. 4:24 is particularly apt because it comes from Moses's speech to the people as they are about to enter the land. Moses himself is not able to enter, and so the audience must persevere and be careful to avoid presumption.

Concluding exhortations (13:1-25)

In form, Hebrews 13 more closely resembles the endings of Paul's letters than do Hebrews 1-12. Here Hebrews spells out the proper mode of "acceptable worship" called for at the end of Hebrew 12, characterized by moral probity, community solidarity, and an emphasis on sacrifice. The admonitions in vv. 1-5 recall various dimensions of the persecution faced by the community. Brotherly love is all the more crucial when external pressures threaten to undermine their solidarity. While it might afford an opportunity to entertain divine messengers, as in the story of Abraham in Gen. 18:1-15 or the Roman myth of Baucis and Philemon, hospitality extended to itinerant missionaries might be abandoned as the welcoming of strangers could draw unwanted attention from local authorities. Prisoners and victims of torture benefit from the empathy of their fellow believers, who are called to remember them "as though" they are themselves undergoing the same hardship. The call for contentment ("free from the love of money") is practical advice for those whose possessions have been plundered (cf. 10:34). The intended result of this moral exhortation is that the audience may say with confidence (quoting Ps. 117:6), "The Lord is my helper; I will not be afraid" (13:6). If the call to remember their leaders and "consider the outcome of their way of life" is an allusion to martyrdom, this reassurance of divine aid and comfort is all the more crucial. "Remembering" is not some dewy-eyed feeling of nostalgia; instead, as the Greek syntax suggests, it takes the form of imitating their faith (13:7).

Jesus's constancy—"the same yesterday and today and forever" (v. 8; cf. 1:10-12; possibly a confessional formula according to Lane 1991: 502)—contrasts with the "strange teachings" that may harm them, of which Hebrews's author mentions dietary regulations as one example (v. 9; the danger of "drifting away" [2:1] has accelerated to the point where they may be "carried away"). Such teachings do not yield the benefits available to the audience, which has access to an altar not open to priests of the former covenant who were permitted to eat of the sacrifices except on Yom Kippur (v. 10). Given the allusions to Jesus's suffering, the "altar" is less likely a metaphor or metonym for a Eucharistic meal than for Jesus's self-offering, though the cross is not properly speaking an altar since sacrifices are never slaughtered there (Moffitt 2011). Despite the qualitative superiority of his sacrifice, Jesus suffered "outside the city gate" just as the animals sacrificed in the tabernacle were burned "outside the camp" in accordance with the directives in Torah (vv. 11-12; cf. Lev. 6:30; 16:27). For this reason, they should not consider themselves exempt from bearing the abuse he endured. Their willingness to leave the city, whether literally or in some figurative sense, will demonstrate their awareness that there is no "lasting city" on earth for them—perhaps a veiled allusion to Rome, which was already called "the eternal city" in the first century—but, like Abraham (Heb. 11:10), that they are awaiting a home in heaven (13:13-14). In the meantime, they should continually offer a "sacrifice of praise," be it in the form of good works or a confession of faith (vv. 15-16). The author thus employs "thoroughly cultic language to make a deeply uncultic statement" (Klauck 1992: 890). Critiques of animal sacrifice in the Old Testament demand that it be accompanied by a humble heart and obedience to Torah (Ps. 51:6; Isa. 1:11; Jer. 7:21-23; Hos. 6:6; Amos 5:21-24; Mic. 6:6-8), while Greco-Roman writers such as Plutarch and Lucian of Samosata often mock cultic practices for being ridiculous and undignified or for the mistaken views they reflect either about the dependence of the gods on human offerings or the efficacy of such rites in the face of an inexorable fate that governs all things.

The closing benediction (Heb. 13:20-21) is replete with motifs appearing earlier in the letter and also with distinctive expressions implied but never stated directly elsewhere in the course of the author's argument. It contains the only unambiguous references to the resurrection of Jesus as distinct from his exaltation to heaven and the right hand of God. Other references to resurrection are made to the risings of other individuals (11:19, 35) or to the general resurrection of the faithful in the eschaton, as is likely the case with the inclusion of "resurrection of the dead [plural]" among the "basic" teachings in Heb. 6:1-2. Here one also finds the image of Jesus as a shepherd that is developed more fully in the Fourth Gospel (10:1-18; cf. Mt. 18:10-14; Lk. 15:3-7; 1 Pet. 2:25; 5:4). If it is an echo of Isa. 63:11-14 LXX, where similar language is applied to Moses, then the addition of the qualifier "great" may be intended to present Jesus as a second Moses superior to the first one (Bruce 1990: 378–88). The blood of this shepherd establishes a new covenant (9:15-20; 10:19, 29), now described as "eternal." It is also noteworthy that Jesus is called "Lord," a title usually reserved for God in Hebrews (7:21; 8:2, 8-11; 10:16, 30; 12:5-6, 14; 13:6; the ascription of "glory" to Jesus instead of God is likewise striking).

This benediction appears in between two brief sets of final instructions (13:17-19, 22-25). The audience is to submit to the authority of the community leaders "with joy and not with sighing," perhaps an insinuation that malcontents are channeling the spirit of insubordination at work in the grumbling of the Israelites upset with Moses's leadership in the desert. Speaking in the first-person singular, the subsequent request for prayer and declaration of a clear conscience indicate that the author himself is to be numbered among these leaders. His desire to be reunited with them in the near future and his mention of Timothy are reminiscent of Pauline letter endings. Manuscript evidence does not support the conjecture that this postscript was added by someone other than the author so as to convince later readers that it came from Paul (though see Rothschild 2009 for the early reception of Hebrews as Pauline).

Is the author's comment that he has spoken briefly in his "word of exhortation" an example of self-deprecating irony or is it a reminder that he still has much more to say (cf. 5:11; 11:32)? As a letter, Hebrews is hardly brief. As a homily or sermon like those delivered in Hellenistic synagogues, it is perhaps more typical (cf. 2 Macc. 15:8-11; Acts 13:15; Wills 1984). Reading it aloud might take forty-five minutes or so, depending on the speed and style of the person "delivering" it. Other early Christian authors making similar remarks about the brevity of their letters are in fact more concise than Hebrews (1 Pet. 5:12; Ignatius, *Rom.* 8:2; *Pol.* 7:3; the *Epistle of Barnabas*, however, is much longer but nonetheless presents itself as "short" [1:5]). In relaying the good news of Timothy's release from captivity, the author also sends a subtle message that he plans to visit in the near future when he can continue his instruction and gauge their responsiveness to his message.

3

The Holy Spirit in Hebrews

In Heb. 12:2 the author provides an apt summary of the aim of his entire sermon when he tells the audience to keep their eyes on Jesus. He asks his audience to consider—deeply consider—who Jesus is and what he has done. This will shape their view of the God of Israel, their understanding of their own community, and will ultimately determine how they live. The author begins with a Christological paradox: Jesus is exalted as high as God (Hebrews 1) yet has been lowered even to the point of human death (Hebrews 2). Because he has done so and lived, and because the audience has confessed it to be true, they are members of him and on their way to dwell with God forever (Hebrews 3–4). This is the basic story the author has to tell.

From here the author turns to more specific details, specifically concerning the nature of Jesus as priest (Hebrews 5). He mediates between the people and God as did former priests, but his priesthood is radically different. After an interlude serving to warn the audience that they are entering difficult territory and that they may lack the spiritual preparation for it, the author forges ahead, confident in their previous faithfulness and in God's desire to lead them into a deeper understanding of the basis for their hope in this priest (Hebrews 6). Melchizedek is the first parallel drawn from Israel's Scriptures (Hebrews 7), followed by the New Covenant (Hebrews 8) and the sacrificial system (Hebrews 9–10). Jesus's priesthood gives them access to God, and so they must not squander their faith in him (Hebrews 10). The previous struggles of faith from Israel's past serve as exemplars that all point to the faith Jesus displayed and makes possible (Hebrews 11). He instructs them about the divine discipline that will guide them to God's dwelling forever (Hebrews 12). Until that kingdom fully arrives, they need to know how to live in light of who they now know God to be as revealed in the great shepherd and king-priest, Jesus (Hebrews 13).

The exposition in the preceding chapters alerts the reader to many of the critical issues raised by the epistle, but we have devoted space here to conversations about references to the Holy Spirit in Hebrews for two reasons. First, pneumatology is part of the cutting-edge debate among scholars who study the author's broader theology. Several scholars discussed here will continue to develop this line of research in the next several years. As New Testament scholars turn their attention to the ways in which various texts have contributed to the development of Christian orthodoxy, the Holy Spirit will be among the aspects of Hebrews ripe for examination. Second, focus on the Holy Spirit also helps us better understand the historical context of Hebrews. The understanding of God's Spirit is one of the fascinating differences between early Jewish thought and nascent Christian teaching. As a bridge between the two communities, Hebrews gives insights into the ways in which some first-century Jewish communities were coming to understand God and the Spirit of God in light of what they believed about Jesus. The Holy Spirit's connection to Israel's Scriptures in this document is one of the most important motifs for understanding that transitional period.

Father, Son, and Holy Spirit

Hebrews applies many titles to Jesus: Son of God, high priest, mediator, pioneer, and perfecter of the faith, the great shepherd of the sheep. The belief that Jesus is the Messiah reorients the author's understanding of the God of Israel in light of his life, death, and resurrection. The book opens with a reflection on Jesus's status as Son and dwells at length on his filial relationship with God the Father. Doctrinally-minded readers may sense something missing in the Christological and theological portrait found in Hebrews. God the Father and Jesus the Son are present throughout Hebrews, but references to the Holy Spirit seem sparse by comparison. "Spirit" (*pneuma*) appears twelve times, seven of which refer to the Holy Spirit or Spirit of God (2:4; 3:7; 6:4; 9:8, 14; 10:15, 29). With so few references, it is not surprising that scholars have found relatively little material for reconstructing the sermon's pneumatology. As Jack Levison has documented, scholars of an earlier period tended to frame the issue in stark terms (2016: 90–91). Henry B. Swete categorically ruled out Hebrews from his book on New Testament pneumatology: "In Hebrews there is no theology of the Spirit" (1910: 249). Barnabas Lindars likewise asserts that "the Spirit plays no part in the argument of the letter" (1991: 56). More measured is the conclusion drawn by Anthony C. Thiselton: so few references in such a substantial work as Hebrews "raises a question about those who seem to claim that a genuine Christian will speak constantly about the Holy Spirit" (2013: 156).

While a robust pneumatology is not to be found in every early Christian writing, in recent years several scholars have argued that Hebrews has more to say about the Holy Spirit than has previously been recognized. Martin Emmrich begins his exploration of this "nearly uncharted territory" by placing Hebrews's references to God's spirit alongside contemporaneous Jewish literature (2003b: vii; cf. Emmrich 2002a; 2003a). His analysis discovers both resonance and departure. He arranges the references in Hebrews thematically along a spectrum, from those most similar to mainstream Jewish pneumatology to those that are most distinctive. On one end of this spectrum, the author of Hebrews, like other Jewish writers of the time, links the spirit of holiness with the priestly office. Also similar are the connections between God's Spirit and God's Word. On this point, however, Emmrich argues that the ways in which Hebrews describes the Holy Spirit both orating and interpreting Jewish texts is without parallel. He treats two of the warning passages (Heb. 2:4; 6:4) under the rubric "guide of the eschatological exodus" and likewise finds similarities and differences. Like many other Jewish texts, Hebrews views God's Spirit as retributive; in other words, "the (possession/) retention of the Spirit is contingent on obedience" (2003a: 74). But because the Spirit is linked to Christ's once-for-all sacrifice, the forfeiture of the Spirit cannot be undone. Emmrich argues that this aspect of the author's thought is "absolutely unique" among Jews and Christians of the same period and that it makes a seminal contribution to the pneumatology of the early church (2003a: 89). The Spirit is the Spirit of the God of Israel, but Hebrews's presentation of the Spirit is thoroughly eschatological in that the Spirit is dependent on the advent of the Messiah Jesus.

David Allen (2008; 2009) attends to the letter's references to the divine spirit and finds that this dimension of the recipients' reality has been underappreciated. He suggests that a Pentecostal lens allows the interpreter to see more clearly how the Spirit pervades their experience. Although the experience is mentioned only once, the reception of the Spirit and the accompanying signs (2:4) influence the remainder of the author's exhortation to the community, most conspicuously in a handful of other passages that in his reading describe the Holy Spirit (6:1-2, 4; 9:8, 14; 10:29). In addition to the power of God and the voice of Scripture, Allen sees the Holy Spirit as the mediator of revelation (2009: 55). He concludes that "the spirit is also the one whose very presence and reception testifies to the inauguration of the new covenant dispensation" (2009: 63). Allen acknowledges that it is improper to assume that the author thinks in explicitly or full-fledged trinitarian categories but contends that, in describing the Spirit as an agent, the author helps to propel later Christian thinkers along a trinitarian path that will lead to Chalcedon and beyond (2009: 53).

Stephen Motyer goes beyond the position staked out by Allen's to argue that Hebrews is "certainly congruent with a 'trinitarian' approach to the Spirit, and might even contribute something distinctive" to the range of New Testament teachings on the topic (2012: 214). After surveying Hebrews's portrayal of Israel's Scriptures as "spirit-empowered prophetic interpretation," he focuses on the reference to the eternal spirit in Heb. 9:14 (2012: 226). It is only at this point, he argues, that the connection between Christ and the Spirit becomes explicit. Motyer's treatment of the references to the Spirit in Hebrews convinces him of a congruence between Hebrews and later Christian orthodoxy by showing the "inseparability of Christ and the Spirit" (2012: 216). Because the Spirit is connected with the flesh of Christ, there is a foundation for the kind of "spiritual discipleship *in the flesh*" which the author subsequently expounds in Hebrews 11–13 (2012: 227).

In his essay in a volume that presents a biblical theology of the Holy Spirit, Alan K. Hodson organizes the references to the Holy Spirit in a covenantal scheme: the need for, inauguration of, and authentication of the new covenant (2014: 227). Hebrews regards the Holy Spirit as the author of texts that show the need for a new covenant, sees the connection between the Holy Spirit and the new salvation through the death and resurrection of Christ, and therefore asserts "dire consequences" (Hodson 2014: 232) for anyone who rejects the work of the Spirit. Hence, it is the presence of the Spirit that indicates a person's standing in the new covenant people. Hodson argues that in Hebrews, the Spirit is both personal and divine. This is evident by the Spirit's participation with the work of God the Father in interpreting Scripture and with Christ in procuring salvation. Whereas it may not be articulated as explicitly or in the same terms, Hodson nevertheless claims that Hebrews's pneumatology is no less developed than Paul's or Luke's.

Jack Levison counters the view that Hebrews has no theology of the Spirit by calling into question certain presuppositions upon which it is based (2016). In order to explain why they find Hebrews pneumatologically tepid, it is insufficient to consult a concordance and tally up the number of times "spirit" is mentioned. Levison argues that Hebrews does have a coherent theology of the Spirit that is integral to the letter's argument. In Hebrews, the Spirit is not simply the source or the "inspirer" of the text of the Scriptures that breathes life into them. Earlier scholars have recognized as much. Rather, the Holy Spirit in Hebrews is active in the process of interpreting, adapting, and extending Scripture for the present community, as one sees throughout the letter (3:7-8; 9:8; 10:15). Editorial expansions, altered citations, and the use of the present tense are among the forms in which this process unfolds, wherein "the primary locus of inspiration is not the ancient text but the contemporary community" (2016: 97). In other passages that appear to refer to the Spirit, (2:4; 6:4; 9:14; 10:29), the author embeds contemporary concerns in ancient traditions, often in a way that recalls other New Testament texts in which the Spirit appears, such as the Pentecost story in Acts (2016: 101–5). In addition, the Spirit is directly connected to salvation in Hebrews, including the way it unfolds and the need for perseverance in achieving it fully. A number of references occur in the passages warning the readers about the possibility of drifting away from the salvation declared by Jesus. Even those that do not nonetheless describe key features of salvation, such as the manner in which it compensates for the inability of the institutions of the former covenant to purify believers from sin. Levison makes a convincing argument that close attention to the Spirit's function in the letter provides a valuable window into the experience and belief of the early church.

Madison N. Pierce focuses on the author's citation of Ps. 95:7-11 and argues that the most cohesive reading of Heb. 3:7–4:11 acknowledges that the Spirit is the primary divine actor in this section and in the letter as a whole (2017). The author characterizes the Spirit in particular ways by having him speak this particular text to this flesh-and-blood community, and "their obedience or disobedience serves as their nonverbal reaction to the Spirit's testimony" (2017: 179). Pierce believes it is important to recognize that the Spirit in Hebrews does not simply serve as a medium for the words of Scripture spoken by God the Father but possesses agency as the source and speaker of those words. Along with Jewish traditions of which the author of Hebrews seems aware, he sees the same guidance of the Holy Spirit experienced by the wilderness generation of old as available to the first-century community of "Hebrews," be they Jewish or Gentile, who are on their own journey in the wilderness. This is a powerful role, in which the Spirit is depicted as "one who guides and as one who offers rest to the faithful or retribution to the unfaithful" (2017: 182).

As this cursory review makes clear, the Holy Spirit is no longer neglected in the secondary literature devoted to Hebrews. The commentary in the preceding chapter highlights two motifs as they arise in the course of the author's exposition, namely, the portrayal of the Spirit speaking Israel's Scriptures and the association of the Spirit with the work of salvation. There is an emerging consensus among scholars that these two areas merit more detailed attention.

The Holy Spirit and divine speech

"One cannot help but wonder," writes Alan Mitchell, "if such an accomplished author . . . did not have a special appreciation of God as a communicator" (2007: 40). This aspect of Hebrews is manifest from the opening verses, where the author describes God's disclosure of the divine plan through speech: "God has spoken . . . through a Son" (1:2). When he introduces citations of Israel's Scriptures, he typically does so with verbs of speech. In most cases, it is stated or implied that God is speaking the Scriptures (1:5, 6, 7, 8-12, 13; 4:3; 5:5, 6; 6:14; 7:17, 21; 8:8-12; 10:30, 37-38; 11:18; 12:5-6, 26). But the author gives the Holy Spirit a voice in two noteworthy passages.

The first occurs in the author's exhortation based on his multiple citations of Psalm 95 in Heb. 3:7–4:11. He encourages his readers to assume their standing as members of God's household (3:6) by listening to the words of the Holy Spirit—"as the Holy Spirit says" (3:7). Within the quotation from the psalm, the Holy Spirit urges listeners to be responsive to the voice of God who, almost imperceptibly, appropriates the words of the cited text. "Today if you hear *his* voice" in v. 7 becomes, without any indication of a change of speaker, "they saw my works . . . [and] I was angry . . . and I said" in vv. 9-10.

Without any indication to mark a change of speaker, the Holy Spirit is again presented as speaking the first two phrases of the citation in v. 15 for similar hortatory purposes. This conjunction between the speech of God and of the Holy Spirit continues in Hebrews 4 where the author parses various phrases from the psalm he is citing. The line from Ps. 95:11 that is attributed earlier to the Holy Spirit—"As he [God? the Holy Spirit?] has said, 'As in *my* anger I swore, they will not enter *my* rest'"—is repeated, apparently in reference to God, whose works "were finished at the foundation of the world" (4:3). The same ambiguity is found in v. 4: "For he [God? the Holy Spirit?] has somewhere [Gen. 2:2] spoken . . . 'And God rested on the seventh day'" (RSV; the NRSV attempts to smooth over the difficulty by rendering it "in one place it speaks"). In v. 5 the Greek has no introductory formula, though it should perhaps be supplied from the previous verse: "He said, 'They shall never enter *my* rest'" (RSV; the NRSV is more literal here: "And again . . ."). Finally, "through David" in v. 7 "he" repeats the warning about hardening their hearts. With quotations inside quotations inside still other quotations, it is difficult to follow exactly who might be speaking in these passages. The turns are almost dizzying—one imagines the difficulty of sorting it out in an oral-aural setting. Whether or not it is the author's intention to disorient the attentive reader, this manner of citing Scripture leaves the impression that God and this "Holy Spirit" speak in harmony.

The second occurrence of the Holy Spirit speaking a text evidences a similar distinction in unity. The author cites Jer. 31:31-34 in Heb. 8:8-12. When he cites it a second time in Hebrews 10, it is the Holy Spirit who "witnesses to us": "He has said, 'This is the covenant *I* will make with them after those days, says the Lord: *I* will put *my* laws in their hearts, and *I* will write them on their minds, . . . and *I* will remember their sins and lawless deeds no more'" (10:15-17). If it is the case that the Holy Spirit can voice the words of God, can proclaim the words of Jeremiah, and speak "through David" (4:7), then when God spoke to the fathers in the prophets long ago, it is in, through, with, and alongside the Holy Spirit. For Hebrews, the citations of Psalm 95 and Jeremiah 31 demonstrate that just as God speaks through the prophets, so too does the Spirit.

Hebrews carefully constructs these conversations in such a way that the speech of God and the Spirit's speech manifest (rather than explicate in a discursive manner) a web of relationships among agents regarded as divine. One may infer from the author's clear affirmation of the Holy Spirit's speech in the Hebrew Scriptures that he regards it to be present in the speech acts of God that identify and establish Jesus as Son and, accordingly, God as Father (e.g., 2 Sam. 7:14 and Ps. 2:7, quoted in Heb. 1:5). The scriptural speaking of the Holy Spirit means that the author's opening chapter may be more fertile soil for pneumatological reflection than the explicit Father/Son language seems to warrant at first glance. In choosing these spoken texts to demonstrate this relationship, the author conceives of the Spirit as somehow participating in the bond between the Father and the Son. The familial relationship through which the identity of God comes to expression, then, is not only a paternal/filial relationship but is, at the same time, in the hermeneutic of Hebrews, a pneumatological one as well.

The Holy Spirit and human salvation

Humans come to participate in this relationship by virtue of their membership in the household of God (3:1-6). But how does one become a child of God? Does Hebrews believe that humans have always existed as God's children, simply by virtue of their status as part of the creation? Did God take the members of Israel as children when he covenanted with Abraham or affirmed their calling to be a "priestly kingdom" through Moses at Sinai? And what about Gentiles who may join the fold? Hebrews leaves no doubt about the reality of the family relation. Without any such explicit language of adoption as is found in Paul (Rom. 8:15; Gal. 4:5; Eph. 4:5), however, the reader of Hebrews is left to wonder about the mechanism. How, precisely, does Jesus become their brother and God their Father? Indeed, to the extent that the identities of the believer and of Jesus are disclosed in the Scriptures and actualized by the "living and active" word of God (4:12) encountered there, according to Hebrews, the Holy Spirit is therefore active in the creation of the family of God.

The author of Hebrews reminds them of their status immediately after explaining how and why Jesus had to become "like his brothers and sisters" to be "the pioneer of their salvation" (2:10, 17) and just before allowing the Holy Spirit to present the negative example of the children of Israel (3:7–4:11). A further difference between the wilderness generation and those who now enjoy a sibling relationship with Jesus is that the former did not have access to the sanctuary of "the greater and perfect tent" and could only offer up sacrifices that could not perfect the conscience (9:6-14). According to Heb. 9:8, the Holy Spirit not only "indicates" or "makes manifest" (*dēlountos*) this set of affairs but also acts as the means by which it is set right: "the blood of Christ, who through the eternal Spirit offered himself up without blemish to God, [purifies] our conscience from dead works to worship the living God" (9:14; a number of ancient manuscripts replace "eternal" with "holy").

Hence, inasmuch as the words enshrined in Scripture place the Spirit at the inauguration of the divine relationship between Father and Son in Hebrews, the Spirit's work secures and sustains the divine-human relationship.

*   *   *

Interest in Hebrews's pneumatology shows no signs of waning as scholars reconsider the dismissive view that the letter has little or nothing to say about the Holy Spirit. The distinct yet unified work of God and the Spirit are on display, especially in such passages as Heb. 3:7–4:11, in a manner which enabled the early church, by means of "prosopological exegesis," to read the one God as multiple "persons" (*prosōpon; persona*) in the biblical text. Matthew Bates observes that this way of reading ultimately endowed the metaphor of "person" seemingly embedded in its assumptions a "privileged status as the premier category for conceptualizing and expressing differentiation within the one God," especially after the fourth-century councils of Nicaea and Constantinople (2015: 175). Historical-critical exegesis, in concert with studies in the early reception history, holds great promise for elucidating the teaching of Hebrews because the former pre-empts anachronistic hermeneutical strategies while the latter supplies exegetical clues—gleaned from thinkers much closer to the language and thought-world of the original author and audience—that are often overlooked by modern interpreters. In so doing, commentators are better able to reconstruct the author's conception of a relational God.

4

The Reception History of Hebrews

Chapter outline

Relative to the Gospels and Paul's letters, the Epistle to the Hebrews remained below the radar of most scholars for much of the twentieth century. Since the birth of biblical studies as a critical discipline in the early modern period, scholars have trained their attention primarily on what has been called "the world behind the text." This phrase refers to the constellation of historical, social, cultural, and political circumstances that contribute to the composition of a text, with special reference to the flesh-and-blood author and the original audience. While this focus is necessary in order to forestall anachronistic readings of the biblical text, it has sometimes overshadowed the diverse interpretations of and responses to the text by poets, musicians, artists, and other "ordinary" readers. The variety of readings of Hebrews is itself a testimony to the richness of the original text. This longer history of reception both inside and outside the academy and the church—what Germans refer to as the history of its "effects," or *Wirkungsgeschichte*—features a number of fascinating highlights as interpreters have wrestled with its challenging exposition (Heen and Krey 2005; Torgerson 2011; Laansma and Treier 2012; Rittgers 2017).

Hebrews 1

The opening chapter of Hebrews appears frequently alongside John 1 in Christmas liturgies and lectionaries readings on account of its poetic probing of the mystery of the Incarnation. Church fathers and Reformers alike delight in detailing the "many and various ways" in which God had communicated, be it in an all-night wrestling match with Jacob, a burning bush with Moses, or a smoke-filled temple with Isaiah. Hymn writers have extolled "Fairest Lord Jesus" for the way he "shines brighter . . . than all the angels heaven can boast," and Handel sets Heb. 1:5 to music in part two of his *Messiah*.

More commonly, however, the opening verses have served as a theological battleground (Young 1969; Greer 1973). Above all, Christology has overshadowed the abstruse debates about angelology based on the latter half of the chapter. Practically every Christological controversy of the first several Christian centuries turned on the manner in which certain clauses of the exordium or introduction have been understood. The key term *hypostasis* in Heb. 1:3, usually translated "substance," provides the vocabulary used in many debates. Sabellianism, for example, taught that there is one God, an indivisible monad, and that the three persons of the Trinity are three separate "modes" in which the one God is made manifest, though not all at the same time. For this reason, Sabellians are often called Modalists, and many of their teachings are found today in Oneness Pentecostalism. They agreed with Trinitarian teaching that God and Jesus were of the same substance but were puzzled by Hebrews's teaching that, according to v. 3, Jesus could sit down at the Father's side and still be "the exact imprint of God's very being." Patristic writers also use this verse repeatedly in disputes with the Arians to prove that Jesus is *homoousios*, "of the same substance," with the Father and therefore fully divine. Arians further claimed that Jesus was "made," not "begotten," and refused to recognize Hebrews as canonical on account of this disagreement. Theologians who affirmed the Nicene Creed likewise found a warrant for the description of Jesus as "light from light" in Hebrews's reference to the "brightness of his glory" (KJV; cf. Athanasius *C. Ar.* 3:65; Basil of Caesarea, *Hex.* 9:6; Gregory of Nyssa, *C. Eun.* 2:11). Adoptionists identified either Jesus's "appointment" as heir or his ascension to heaven in vv. 3-4 when he "became" superior to the angels as the moment when Jesus became the Son, to which it was countered that the "begetting" of v. 5 is qualitatively different from adoption. In more recent times, the New World Translation produced by the Jehovah's Witnesses substitutes "obeisance" for the "worship" used in all other major translations, in line with their belief that Jesus is another name for the archangel Michael and thus undeserving of the honor due to God.

Surveying these debates, Cyril of Jerusalem (*Catech.* 16:24) counsels, "Let us be content with this knowledge [that there is Father, Son, and Holy Spirit] and not busy ourselves with questions about the divine nature or hypostasis." For much of antiquity, his advice was more honored in the breach than in the observance.

Hebrews 2

The relationship of Father to the Son also occupies interpreters of Hebrews 2, as do "the gifts of the Holy Spirit" (2:4). "Continuationists" and "cessationists" have both appealed to Heb. 2:3-4 on the question of miracles and other spiritual gifts such as speaking in tongues and whether they came to an end with the close of the apostolic age. Emphasis on the proclamation of the word over the sacraments leads Protestant Reformers like Heinrich Bullinger to see this passage as particularly relevant to their role as preachers and to underscore the way in which clear doctrine renders miracles superfluous (Rittgers 2017: 31–33).

Theological anthropology has attracted much of the attention devoted to Heb. 2:5-18. Hebrews has both good news and bad news to share on this score. The Council of Trent (Denzinger and Schönmetzer 1963: 1511) quotes Heb. 2:14 and declares anathema those who deny that Adam's transgression, and therefore original sin, entails captivity to the one who has "the empire of death," that is, the devil. But by the same token, in response to Apollinarianism, which taught that Christ had taken on human flesh and a "lower" soul but not a human mind, Gregory Nazianzus (*Ep.* 101) cites Heb. 2:17 and the precedent of Jesus becoming like his brothers and sisters "in every respect," explaining that "what has not been assumed has not been healed." Thomas Aquinas concurs that such suffering in human nature was the very point of the Incarnation (*In Heb.* 2.14-18 [139]). Maximus the Confessor (*Or. dom.* 348) puts it in vivid terms: by taking on flesh, Jesus made it poisonous to the devil "in order that he might vomit up all those whom he had swallowed when he held sway." The lengths to which Jesus went to redeem fallen humanity, according to the Apostles' Creed, include the "descent in hell," which the Catholic Catechism (§§635–636) understands as the occasion on which he "conquered death and the devil and freed those who all their lives were held in slavery by the fear of death" (Heb. 2:14-15; cf. §632 on Heb. 13:20). Others also see an allusion to Christ's descent into hell during the triduum on Holy Saturday in Heb. 2:7-9, where he is made "for a little while lower than the angels," though the Heidelberg Catechism §44, citing Heb. 5:7-10, says this means only that he delivered us "from the anguish and torment of hell." A number of ancient scribes further complicate this discussion by producing manuscripts that depict Christ tasting death for everyone "apart from God" instead of "by the grace of God."

Hebrews 3–4

Trinitarian debates figure prominently also in Hebrews 3, with Arians inferring from the "appointment" of Jesus in vv. 1-6 that Jesus must be a creature of the God who created him and to whom he was faithful. Over against the medieval doctrine of "implicit faith" according to which a Christian believes on authority what the church teaches even in the absence of understanding, John Calvin instead focuses on the "confession" Christians must boldly and explicitly make (Long 2011: 69–80). From the earliest days of the church, the proper interpretation of the Old Testament was of paramount concern, and one case study consulted by many theologians for understanding the relationship between the covenants has been the author's handling of the wilderness generation's story in Heb. 3:7–4:13 (Lee 2016). Equally influential is the manner in which this text informed the Benedictine view of the Christian life as a moral and spiritual journey with rest in heaven as its destination, with the Exodus symbolizing freedom from vice and sin. Seventh-day Adventists teach that the Sabbath discussed in Heb. 4:1-11 is not simply a foreshadowing of the eschatological rest to be enjoyed by all the faithful but, rather, remains a "perpetual memorial" instituted for all humanity to observe on Saturdays ("the seventh day"), not Sundays. God's swearing that the Israelites would not enter his rest and the statement that "his works were finished at the foundation of the world" (3:7; 4:3) supplied grist for theological disputes about predestination in the ninth century between Gottschalk and Rabanus Maurus and later between Calvinists and Arminians (Koester 2001: 31).

The metaphor for the word of God in Heb. 4:12-13 as a "two-edged sword" that "divides soul from spirit, joints from marrow [and] is able to judge the thoughts and intentions of the heart" has proven to be a fertile one for theologians expounding on the distinctive attributes of Scripture. The symbolism of the two edges of the sword is sometimes interpreted as the two testaments (Augustine, *Civ.* 20.21), and the statement that nothing is hidden from God finds its way into arguments for divine omniscience. John Chrysostom observes that the prophets also had to speak of sabers, bows, and other weapons in order to seize the attention of their audiences (*Hom. Heb.* 7:2), as if it were not sufficiently arresting to hear that "all are naked and laid bare to the eyes of the one to whom we must render an account." Calvin shifts metaphors in his commentary on Hebrews: the Word of God is a hammer, and the heart of the unfaithful is like an anvil, "so that its hardness repels its strokes, however powerful they may be." Transcripts of sermons preached in the 1970s at the People's Temple reveal that Jim Jones was fond of quoting Heb. 4:12-13, after which he typically reminded his followers of his own ability to "discern the heart" and even proclaiming on occasion, "I am the Word," in case they did not connect the dots on their own. (Only Jn 14:12 is quoted more often.)

The Council of Chalcedon punctuates its condemnation of the Monophysites for teaching that the human nature had ceased to exist in Christ when the second person of the Trinity assumed it by quoting Heb. 4:15, "like us in all things but sin," and thus "consubstantial with the Father as to his divinity and consubstantial with us as to his humanity." Branch Davidian leader David Koresh taught that a sinless messiah could neither judge nor sympathize with ordinary believers, and so he took on the role of the "sinful messiah" that he thought was prophesied in Ps. 40:12, engaging in activities that led to the death of several dozen members of the Branch Davidian sect in a confrontation at Waco, Texas, in 1993.

Hebrews 5

As early as the *Apostolic Constitutions* of the fourth century and as recently as the Second Vatican Council in the 1960s, Catholic teaching on holy orders draws on the discussion of the high priesthood in Heb. 5:1-6 (*Catechism of the Catholic Church* §§ 1539–1540), as did Jan Hus and other critics of priestly abuses. Melchizedek, who is first mentioned here before receiving detailed treatment in Heb. 7:1-28, becomes embroiled early in the modern period in debates about the relationship between sacred and secular authority. Rulers such as Constans II in the seventh century invoked the example of the priest-king Melchizedek as one who had jurisdiction in both legal and theological matters, as did popes such as Innocent III and Gregory IX in the thirteenth century (Koester 2001: 32). Annotations to the Westminster Confession of Faith XXIII point the reader to Heb. 5:4 lest they forget that a civil magistrate "may not assume to himself the administration of the Word and sacraments, or the power of the keys of the kingdom of heaven." Melchizedek appears in the Book of Mormon as a holy prophet and king (*Alma* 13:14), and the priesthood he exercises there is known to Adam but withdrawn from the people of Israel when they fail to live up to the covenant associated with it. Since the nineteenth century, the president of the Church of Christ of Latter-day Saints has presided over the Melchizedek Priesthood, an order not found elsewhere in the Christian tradition.

Jesus's prayers and "loud cries and tears" in v. 7 receive sustained scrutiny from patristic writers, though in ways that at times come into conflict. Theodore of Mopsuestia (*C. Apollinaris* 3:4), for example, sees Jesus's fear as a sign that his divine nature did not displace his human nature and thereby make the cross easier to endure, but John Chrysostom (*Hom. Heb.* 8:3) suggests that his cries were an "accommodation" whereby he made allowance for the inability of humans to comprehend the divine on its own terms. Similarly, whereas Cyril of Alexandria understands Hebrews to be saying that Jesus played a part, so to speak, weeping in order to suppress our tears and allowing himself to feel fear in order to lend us courage, "even appear[ing] somehow to need a savior and learn obedience," Theodoret responds to Cyril's Tenth Anathema by interpreting the suffering as an anti-Docetic measure of sorts intended to demonstrate that the Incarnation "was not perfected in appearance or seeming" (Heen and Krey 2005: 75). Thomas Aquinas later reconciles the paradox of a Jesus needing to "learn" anything at all by construing it as the hard-won "knowledge of experience" as distinct from abstract understanding (*In Heb.* 5:8-14 [259]).

As for the remedial learning to be done by the audience—the "milk, not solid food" (5:11-14)—Origen helpfully identifies the opening chapters of Genesis and Ezekiel along with the Song of Songs as belonging to the category of writings that should be held back from children and others who may be unready for such hearty spiritual fare (*Comm. Cant.*, prologue).

Reading other Scriptures, however, is mentioned as a means of learning "to distinguish good from evil."

Hebrews 6

The so-called warning passages have perhaps sparked more controversy than any other section of the letter, and none more than the rejection of a "second repentance" in Heb. 6:4-6 (Bateman 2007). Disputes arose as early as the third century. The *Shepherd of Hermas* (*Mand.* 4.3.1-6) alludes to Hebrews when the author tells an angel that "'some teachers' contend that there is no second repentance beyond the one given when we went down into the water and received remission of our former sins." Writing early in his Montanist period, Tertullian echoes Hebrews when criticizing *Hermas*, remarking that the apostles did not allow repentance for post-baptismal sins committed by fornicators and adulterers (*Pud.* 20.5). Novatian in the mid-third century maintains that there are indeed sins for which repentance is impossible, such as the "sin against the Holy Spirit" mentioned in Mt. 12:31. Some orthodox writers are subsequently hesitant to cite Hebrews because of its popularity among the Novatianists and Montanists (Tabbernee 2001). The Decian persecution of 249–250 and its aftermath made the resolution of this theological question no mere academic exercise. Can believers who sacrifice to the Roman gods under threat of torture be re-admitted to the church? While Novatian holds to the rigorist position, Cyprian and other church authorities adopt a softer stance, permitting a single opportunity for penance in cases of apostasy. Ambrose and Gregory Nazianzus read the passage in connection with the sacrament of penance and conclude that only renewal by means of a second baptism is proscribed, not repentance per se.

Martin Luther has qualms about Hebrews because he sees its teaching on repentance as running counter to the "pure" Pauline doctrine of grace, while Ulrich Zwingli and other Reformers defend the author by reading vv. 4-6 as hyperbole. Baptist confessional statements frequently contain "eternal security" language of a sort that is in tension with the possibility of apostasy, an impulse sometimes expressed in the popular slogan that describes the believer as "once saved, always saved." Calvinists likewise stress the doctrine of "the perseverance of the saints," though Calvin himself reconciles the rigor of Hebrews's teaching with the gospel via the doctrine of predestination: God favors only the elect with the spirit of regeneration and not the reprobate. Protestant polemicists charge that the theology of the Mass as a sacrifice violates the prohibition in Heb. 6:6 of "recrucifying" Jesus, whereas Catholics respond that it involves a continuation or re-presentation of Christ's once-for-all sacrifice, not a repetition.

Hebrews 7

Readings of Heb. 7:1-28 are in essence attempts at making sense of Hebrews's own readings of Torah as it pertains to the figure of Melchizedek and the Levitical system of sacrifices. Melchizedek's reappearance in Hebrews after his brief hour upon the stage in Genesis no doubt catalyzed the interpretation of his meal with Abraham as a type of the Mass in both the liturgy and in early and medieval Christian art. Eucharistic prayers in the Roman Rite have mentioned the high priest Melchizedek since the eighth century. The Reformed tradition understands the Lord's Supper differently, as is evident when Chapter XXIX of the Westminster Confession of Faith cites Heb. 7:23-28 in arguing that "the Popish sacrifice of the mass (as they call it) is most abominably injurious to Christ's one, only sacrifice." James Joyce strikes a lighter note in *Ulysses* when a character calls his "unsubstantial lunch" a "rite of Melchizedek." The connection between the Levitical system and the ordained priesthood is elaborated at the Council of Trent with reference to Heb. 7:12 (Mitchell 2007: 24–25).

Melchizedek had already been the subject of much speculation in early Judaism. Patristic authors extend this tradition by making guesses about his identity and background. Justin Martyr (*Dial.* 33) identifies Melchizedek as "priest of the uncircumcision" whose ministry prefigures that of Jesus, who later calls Gentiles to faith. Epiphanius mentions a number of heterodox theories about Melchizedek in the fourth book of his *Panarion*. Some Egyptians teach that he is the Holy Spirit, he says, while the Samaritans claim that he was Shem, a rabbinic tradition countenanced by Jerome. The description that he was without mother or father led some to say he was the son of a harlot but others to say he was an angel or the Son of God. A third-century Gnostic text, Nag Hammadi Codex IX, includes an apocalypse in which Melchizedek first relays special messages to an inner circle of followers and then is revealed to be Jesus himself. Family trees become even more twisted with those who assert that Melchizedek is actually Jesus's father. In his *First Sermon on the Theotokos*, Nestorius considers the comparison of Melchizedek to Christ and reasons that if Christ is divine and has no mother, then it cannot so easily be said that Mary is "the mother of God," though his views are condemned at the Council of Ephesus in 431.

Beyond its exegetical details, Hebrews's typological treatment of Melchizedek and of the Levitical priesthood establishes a precedent for later Christian writers. He is not the first writer, Jewish or Gentile, to employ allegory for making sense of confusing texts. But his practice encourages others to take the same approach to writings from every part of the canon, including what would become the New Testament, whether they present thorny hermeneutical problems or are relatively straightforward on the surface. Allegorical flights of fancy occasionally become untethered from the text in medieval exegesis, yet it could be argued that in the absence of some such means of making Old Testament laws and narratives meaningful and relevant to later (especially Gentile) readers, it is possible that the Jewish Scriptures might not have been retained. In the face of Gnostic challenges to the legitimacy of the Hebrew Bible, this was no idle worry.

Hebrews 8–10

Focusing on the old and new covenants, Hebrews 8–10 have provoked a number of forceful responses in the history of interpretation. The description of the worship and the sanctuary in which it is offered in terms of shadow or symbol and reality (8:5; 9:9; 10:1) invites the sort of typological and allegorical exegesis to which the entire Bible has been subjected in the centuries since its composition. When Melito of Sardis (Eusebius, *Hist. eccl.* 4.26.14) first applies the labels Old and New Testament to the Hebrew Scriptures and the additional books gaining canonical authority among Christians, he does so under the theological influence of Heb. 8:8-13 and its use of the covenant language it quotes from Jer. 31:31-34. (*Testamentum* is the Latin rendering of Greek *diathēkē*, "covenant.")

Especially in the post-Holocaust era, Hebrews's characterization of the first covenant as "obsolete" has drawn criticism for promoting supersessionism, a term usually denoting the idea that God has rejected Israel and replaced it with the church (8:13; Svartvik 2016). Unambiguous expressions of anti-Jewish sentiment informed by Hebrews can be found as early as the second century in the *Epistle of Barnabas* and in many authors throughout the patristic era. Jewish-Christian relations in the present are strongly influenced by the degree to which these readings of Hebrews are thought to misunderstand or misrepresent the author's intended message or the historical setting in which he wrote.

Cultic matters come to the fore in readings of Hebrews 9–10. In his massive commentary on Hebrews, Puritan theologian John Owen counters the sixteenth-century Socinian teaching in the Recovian Catechism that Jesus's death on the cross was not a perfect or satisfactory offering but only a preparatory step to the completion of his sacrificial work in the heavenly sanctuary. Based on the layout of heaven described in Hebrews (7:17-28; 8:1-2; 9:22-23), Seventh-day Adventists believe that Jesus began the first phase of his heavenly ministry upon his ascension but commenced the "investigative judgment" only in 1844 when he entered the "second apartment." Models of the atonement as a penal substitution draw heavily on Heb. 9:13-22, to the consternation of theologians who regard it as primitive and barbaric insofar as it posits a wrathful deity demanding blood sacrifice. Jesus's offering of himself to God in Heb. 9:14 is often invoked to disprove the Patripassianist view that God the Father suffered on Calvary with God the Son. Abbot Suger, who oversaw the rebuilding of the twelfth-century church of Saint-Denis, paraphrases Heb. 9:13-14 when he argues by analogy that if Christ's shed blood is more efficacious than that of animals, then the architectural setting for Christian worship and the implements used should be more resplendent than what preceded it (Panofsky 1979: 65).

Liturgical uses of texts from Hebrews 10 stand side by side with theological analyses and applications to church discipline. The Book of Common Prayer prescribes the reading of v. 1 on Good Friday, while v. 20 is echoed in the Liturgy of Saint James at the presentation of the bread and wine. Mary's *fiat* or submission to God in Lk. 1:38 is compared to Jesus's assent to the divine will in Heb. 10:5-7 in John Paul II's encyclical *Redemptoris Mater*. Opponents of Monotheletism wield Heb. 10:7 to condemn the teaching that Jesus had two natures but only one will at the Sixth Ecumenical Council at Constantinople in 681. Many modern theologians reject the notion of Jesus's preexistence, for which many find support in Heb. 10:5, as "not only irrational but utterly meaningless" (Bultmann 1984: 8). To combat absenteeism, the Heidelberg Catechism §103 deems Heb. 10:24-25 to be a paraphrase of the Fourth Commandment to remember the Sabbath. Finally, Jonathan Edwards and D. H. Lawrence have little in common besides the fact that both use Heb. 10:31—the former adapting it for the title of his famous 1741 sermon "Sinners in the Hands of an Angry God" and the latter quoting it in the first line of his posthumously published poem "The Hands of God," only to capture its ambivalence in the second line: "But it is a much more fearful thing to fall out of them."

Hebrews 11–12

Few verses are as quotable as the definition of faith in Heb. 11:1. Perhaps the earliest instance is found in Clement of Alexandria (*Strom.* 2.2.8-9) when he contrasts Christian epistemology with that of the Greeks who malign faith as worthless, saying that "if you do not believe, you emphatically will not understand either," thereby anticipating Anselm's maxim "faith seeking understanding" (*fides quaerens intellectum*). Thomas Aquinas quotes it in the sections of the *Summa Theologica* devoted to faith and reason and to God's existence and alludes to it in the hymn *Pange Lingua* written for the Solemnity of Corpus Christi ("faith for all defects supplying/when the feeble senses fail"). Dante quotes it in *Paradiso* 24 when he is asked to define faith upon arriving in heaven. Rufinus quotes Heb. 11:6 in the same spirit and remarks that this is why "I believe" stands at the beginning of the Apostle's Creed (*Symb.* 3). Following Luther's lead in making faith the key to salvation, Reformers regularly dwell on this formula. Calvin, however, warns that taking it as a precise definition may cause one to misconstrue the author's message. The underlying question of Heb. 11:3—did the universe have a beginning or not, and was it created from something or from nothing?—is one that continues to occupy physicists and philosophers, even if they do not appeal to it in support of the doctrine of creatio ex nihilo as do many theologians. For Calvin, it expresses the "skillful ordering of the universe" which is "a sort of mirror in which we can contemplate God, who is otherwise invisible" (*Institutes* 1.5.1). The anaphoric style is often imitated, as one sees in the *Instructions* of Pachomius who introduces one example after another of biblical heroes finding God in the most unlikely places with the same phrase—"seek God out" (1.25); in the homilies of Venerable Bede on the Gospels—"according to his human nature" (I, 19); and in the speeches of Martin Luther King, Jr.—"I have a dream."

Virtually every figure in the list has been taken as a type of something else in the history of salvation, including Rahab, whom Hilary of Poitiers (*Trac. myst.* 2.9.154) and Gregory of Elvira (*Trac. Orig.* 139) see as a type of the church. John Chrysostom notes that some find fault for the inclusion of less-than-holy figures like Barak, Samson, and Jephthah (*Hom. Heb.* 27.4). It is their faith which interests Hebrews, he explains, not the rest of their lives. The Syriac *Book of Steps* theorizes that it was partly due to their violent tendencies that God delayed their perfection until the coming of the apostles, and that the significance of the Incarnation can be seen in the fact that God no longer needs to instruct his people to use force (Kitchen 2008). True to his pacifist convictions, by contrast, Quaker founder George Fox highlights how these heroes of faith accomplished such great deeds without "outward instruments of war" (cf. Letter 342 and his *Gospel Truth Demonstrated*). Guessing whom Hebrews has in mind with his anonymous summaries in vv. 33-38 becomes something of a parlor game for ancient writers, who frequently consult Jewish pseudepigrapha and Christian apocryphal works to fill in the background.

The procession of figures from the past in Hebrews 11, culminating with their assembly as a "cloud of witnesses" in Heb. 12:1 to cheer on the faithful, has impressed many readers as an especially dramatic evocation of the communion of saints. This section of Hebrews also supplies the chief metaphor for John Bunyan's 1678 classic of spiritual literature, *The Pilgrim's Progress* (Stranahan 1982). Bunyan cites Hebrews more than any other biblical writing in his autobiography and refers to the "Race of Saints" (cf. 12:2) in the preface of the novel. The account of Abraham in Heb. 11:8-16 had a powerful hold on his imagination, as the patriarch leaves one city to seek another and spends his life in between as a pilgrim. One could see *Pilgrim's Progress* as an extended allegory of the Abraham cycle as epitomized in Hebrews, but it is probably more accurate to think of Bunyan treating Abraham as a prototype whose experience will be recapitulated by all of the faithful. (In *Of Plymouth Plantation*, William Bradford made similar reference to this passage when he described the aspirations of the Plymouth colonists who had come to Massachusetts in 1620 on the Mayflower, and indeed the name "pilgrim" for this group was taken from the KJV translation of Heb. 11:13. The Revised Common Lectionary used by many Protestant denominations in the United States also lists this passage as the epistle reading for July 4.) Whereas earlier conceptions of the Christian life as a journey ordinarily focus on prayer as a means to virtue, like the well-known nineteenth-century hymn "I'm But a Stranger Here," Bunyan emphasizes the hostile and alien aspects of the world when only heaven can be called home. When he was in prison for twelve years after the restoration of the monarchy, he found special comfort in Heb. 11:37-38 and the statement that "the world was not worthy" of the various figures who had endured stonings and other torments on account of their faith.

Many readers have been put off by certain hard teachings contained in Hebrews 12. Its characterization of divine discipline in vv. 4-11 is tantamount to advocating child abuse for some interpreters, though few resort to a psychotherapeutic diagnosis of the author as an abused child who is still enduring the effects of childhood trauma and is now perpetuating the vicious cycle unto the next generation by means of a "poisonous pedagogy" (e.g., Capps 1995: 58–77). Luther balked at the suggestion in Heb. 12:16-17 that the reprobate Esau would have no chance to repent. (Patristic writers normally understood his sin to be gluttony or lack of self-control more generally.) It caused Bunyan unceasing anxiety, according to his autobiography, but his spirit would be refreshed when he continued on to the description of Mount Zion in Heb. 12:22-24.

Hebrews 13

The final chapter contains miscellaneous exhortations and meditations which have been interpreted and appropriated in myriad ways. Visiting prisoners (13:3) is one of the corporal works of mercy in Catholic moral theology. Attempts at delineating the precise requirements of keeping "the marriage bed undefiled" and oneself "free from the love of money" indicates that from the patristic period onward Heb. 13:4-5 could be used to authorize abstinence from childbearing and to proscribe private property (Heen and Krey 2005: 230). The admonition to remember their leaders and to "consider the outcome of their way of life" (v. 7) is often understood as an allusion to the martyrdoms of Stephen and James whose faithfulness they are to emulate. The Westminster Confession of Faith XX cites v. 17 in enjoining submission to "lawful exercise" of power, "whether it be civil or ecclesiastical." Not surprisingly, monastic rules such as the fifth-century *Rule of the Four Fathers* also quote this verse. John Wesley, in Sermon 97, "On Obedience to Pastors," bemoans "how little is this understood in the Protestant world!"

Christological concerns are never far from view. Jesus's full divinity is deduced from the fact that he is "the same yesterday and today and forever" by thinkers from across the theological spectrum (Heb. 13:8; cf. Athanasius, *C. Ar.* 1:36; Cyril of Jerusalem, *Catech.*12:17). It also provides the theme of John Paul II's apostolic letter *Tertio Millennio Adveniente* in preparation for the jubilee year 2000. Unitarians, however, contend that Heb. 13:8 only makes the point that the truth about Jesus is unchanging and says nothing about his supposed divinity, while Mary Baker Eddy in *Science & Health with Key to the Scriptures* applies the phrase to "the divine Principle of healing."

Going "outside the camp" (v. 13) is heard as a call to leave the world and pursue the monastic ideal in seclusion from society by such writers as Isaac of Ninevah (*Ascetical Homilies* 37). In a similar vein, in *The Imitation of Christ* (1.23; 2.1) Thomas à Kempis emphasizes the special effort needed to remain "a stranger and a pilgrim on the earth, . . . for here we have no continuing city" (v. 14). John Wycliffe makes pointed reference to the same verse in criticizing the accumulation of property by monasteries (Koester 2001: 32–33). Brahms strikes a more harmonious note in the libretto of *A German Requiem* by borrowing the line for the title of a piece, "Denn wir haben hie keine bleibende Statt" (For Here We Have No Lasting City) in the sixth movement. The call for "a sacrifice of praise" (v. 15) is commonly taken as an endorsement of congregational hymn signing—but only a cappella, in Campbellite churches, as it specifies "the fruit of lips that confess his name" and not musical instruments—and is excerpted in the Holy Anaphora of the Liturgy of Saint Basil the Great in the Ethiopian Orthodox Church.

For Further Study

Hebrews 1

For which side(s) in the Trinitarian debates of the fourth century and later does the opening chapter furnish support?

How does the characterization of the Son in relation to God in 1:2-3 compare with the characterization of Divine Wisdom in the Book of Wisdom (7:25-26)? Does the author appear to be making a conscious allusion to this text?

To what extent is the eschatological urgency implied in the declaration that God has spoken through Jesus "in these last days" (Heb. 1:2) sustained throughout the letter?

In 1:3 the author makes the first of several allusions to Psalm 110 (cf. 1:13; 8:1; 10:12; 12:2). Do these citations serve similar or different functions in their immediate literary context? And how do they compare with the use of Psalm 110 by other New Testament authors (e.g., Mt. 22:44; Acts 2:34-35; Eph. 1:20; 1 Pet. 3:22)?

How might one assess the claim that 1:5-14 is evidence of a form of angel worship against which the author is warning his audience?

Hebrews 1 clearly extols the greatness of the Son. In so doing, what does it say about the nature or character of God the Father?

Hebrews 2

Although it is obscured by the NRSV translation of 2:6-8, the quotation of Ps. 8:4-6 contains singular pronouns. Should the author's use of this psalm be understood anthropologically (i.e., as referring to humans generally) or Christologically (i.e., as referring to Jesus)? How does the answer to this exegetical question relate to one's reading of the larger argument?

The author gives several reason why Jesus "for a little while was made lower than the angels" (2:9). What are these reasons? Are they unique to Hebrews or do they parallel reasons given by other writers? Does Hebrews simply repeat in prose form the poetic description of Jesus's "emptying out" found in Phil. 2:5-11?

Does 2:10 suggest that Jesus bore some imperfection that he had to overcome? "Perfection" is a pervasive motif in Hebrews (5:9, 14; 6:1; 7:11, 19, 28; 9:9-11; 10:1, 14; 11:40; 12:20, 23). Do any senses of *teleios*—for example, "mature," "perfect," "fulfilled," "complete"—seem more fitting than others in the context of the author's argument?

Is it more appropriate to speak of Hebrews espousing a "high" or a "low" Christology (cf. 2:8-9, 15-18; 5:7-10; 12:4-11)?

In 2:10, the NRSV says that God is "bringing many *children* to glory." The Greek text actually says *huioi*, "sons." Is "children" a fitting translation or are their potential meanings lost when the language becomes gender inclusive? If so, what possible meanings does this translation obscure?

Hebrews 3

Traditions about the Israelites of the wilderness generation, first narrated in the Pentateuch, accent different aspects of the story. Some emphasize the rebellion of the people while others highlight the miraculous provision of food, the intimacy of the relationship between the Lord and the people, Moses's leadership qualities, or the heroism of Joshua and Caleb. How does the critique in 3.7–4:11 compare with other accounts (e.g., Ps. 78:5-66; 105:37-45; 106:6-33; CD 3:7-19; Acts 7:35-46; 1 Cor. 10:1-13)?

The author compares Moses the servant (v. 5) to Jesus the Son (v. 6). What are the possible points of comparison and contrast with this image of God's household (vv. 2, 5, 6)?

Sēmeron, "today," appears multiple times in in this section (3:7, 13, 15; 4:7). What are some possible meanings for this term as the author utilizes it here? What might it teach about his conception of time?

Hebrews 4

Jesus "in every respect" has been tested as we are, "yet without sin" (4:15). To what different uses do other New Testament authors put the notion of Jesus's sinlessness (2 Cor. 5:21; 1 Pet. 2:22; 1 Jn 3:5)?

The author states that "a Sabbath rest still remains for the people of God" (4:9) and urges his readers, "Let us therefore make every effort to enter that rest" (4:11). What eschatological implications reverberate in his concept of "Sabbath rest"? Do his instructions here have any bearing on this community's faith practices (cf. 10:25)?

In what ways do the scriptural citations in Hebrews exhibit the qualities ascribed to "the word of God" in 4:12?

Hebrews 5

Melchizedek is first mentioned in 5:5-6. In what way(s) does this first reference anticipate the fuller treatment of Melchizedek in 7:1-28?

In the description of Jesus's suffering in 5:7, does the author presuppose a familiarity with the story of Jesus's agony in Gethsemane? Is it a more general allusion to his suffering on the cross? And in what sense does Jesus "learn obedience through what he suffered" (5:8), especially in light of the author's previous claim that he is without sin? Does this imply that he was not previously "obedient"?

The grammar and syntax of 5:7 are somewhat ambiguous. It has been read as indicating that Jesus was heard *because of* his *eulabeia* ("fear" or "reverence") and also as stating that he was *delivered from* his *eulabeia*. Does Hebrews regard fear of death or fear of God as blameworthy and thus to be avoided?

What does 5:11–6:2 suggest about the nature of early Christian catechesis?

Hebrews 6

Does the warning in 6:4-6 apply to all post-baptismal sin or only to deliberate acts of apostasy? Do other passages in Hebrews give any clues? If it is apostasy, in the absence of any attested "official" persecution, what form might "falling away" take? Is there any indication that the author might have in mind certain "unforgivable" sins like blasphemy (Mk. 3:28-29; 1 Jn 5:16-17)? Is he speaking in hyperbole for rhetorical effect?

In what way does the reference to Gen. 22:17 and the Aqedah (the binding of Isaac) reinforce the argument in 6:13-14?

If Jesus is a "forerunner on our behalf" (6:19-20), does this imply that humans are to follow in his footsteps by, for example, dying a shameful, undeserved death and being exalted to serve at God's right hand?

In 6:15, the author states that Abraham obtained the promise, but later he states that Abraham, along with his descendants, did not receive the promises (11:13)? What is the promise in view in Hebrews 6?

Hebrews 7

In 5:11, after his first mention of Melchizedek, the author says he has "much to say that is hard to explain." What is so difficult about his message as he articulates it in Hebrews 7? Is it intellectually "hard" or is it difficult in some other way?

What interpretive assumptions does the author make in his discussion of Melchizedek and the high priesthood of Jesus? How does the author arrive at the striking claims he makes about Melchizedek (and about Jesus) from the meager information Scripture supplies (Gen. 14:18-20; Ps. 110)?

Where does 7:18 ("the abrogation of an earlier commandment because it was weak and ineffectual") belong on the spectrum of early Christian attitudes about the relationship of Jesus to the law of Moses (cf. Mt. 5:17; Rom. 8:4; Eph. 2:15)?

In what way does Melchizedek—as described by the author—resemble the Son of God (7:3)? Why does he resemble the Son of God and not the other way around?

Hebrews 8

How else might one describe "the main point" of Hebrews from the way the author summarizes it in 8:1-2?

How might one respond to the charge that Hebrews is anti-Semitic or anti-Jewish? Does Hebrews (8:6-7) promote a supersessionist theology? How is the first question different from or similar to the second one?

What is the significance of any differences between the Hebrew text of Jer. 31:31-34, the Septuagint version, and the form in which Hebrews quotes it in 8:8-12?

How does Hebrews's robust description of the "new covenant" compare with the few other uses of "new covenant" language in the New Testament (Lk. 22:20; 1 Cor. 11:25; 2 Cor. 3:6)?

Hebrews 9

Does the argument about the Levitical system of sacrifice make more sense within a pre-70 context or a post-70 context in which the Jerusalem temple has been destroyed?

With which of the various models for the atonement (e.g., satisfaction, penal substitution, ransom/*Christus Victor*, moral influence) does the sacrificial "logic" of Hebrews (esp. 9:11-10:18) fit most comfortably?

Most occurrences of *diathēkē* in Hebrews are translated as "covenant" (e.g., 7:22; 8:6; 9:20; 10:29; 12:24). In 9:16-17, most interpreters understand it as referring to a "last will" or "testament," a usage found in secular Greek literature. If this reading is correct, why does the author shift metaphors?

If it is not correct, how might one understand the passage in continuity with other uses of the term in its "biblical" sense?

Hebrews 10

If the author of the Gospel of John were to see how Hebrews (10:5-7) puts Ps. 40:6-8 on the lips of Jesus, would he recognize it as expressing an understanding of the Incarnation comparable to what one finds in Jn 1:1-18?

Why might members of the community be "neglecting to meet together" (10:25)?

Does the warning against "willfully persisting in sin" in 10:26-31 essentially recapitulate the warnings of 6:4-6 or does it envision a different scenario?

D. H. Lawrence quotes 10:31 in the opening line of his poem "The Hands of God": "It is a fearful thing to fall into the hands of the living God." In the second line he adds, "But it is a much more fearful thing to fall out of them." Does Lawrence grasp the meaning of Hebrews, does he miss it, or is he simply playing with words out of context?

The author urges his readers to be among "those who have faith and so are saved" (10:39). Saved from what—does the author give any indication, here or elsewhere in the book?

Hebrews 11

"Substance," "evidence," "confidence," "assurance," "conviction," "proof"— how does the choice of English words for translating the key terms of the famous definition of faith in 11:1 influence (or reflect) one's understanding of its importance for the author? Does the author have anything specific in mind in referring to "things not seen"?

Faith "in" or "of" Jesus Christ—if Hebrews 11 were factored into the *pistis Christou* debate, which understanding of faith would it support? Is Jesus an example of faith, an object of faith, or both?

Which figures are the most surprising to appear on the "roll call of faith"? Are there any noteworthy or unexpected omissions? In terms of form and function, how does Hebrews 11 compare with other lists of exemplary figures from ancient Jewish literature (e.g., Sirach 44-50; Wis. 10:1-21; 1 Macc. 2:51-60; 4 Macc. 16:16-23; 18:11-19; 4 Ezra 7:105-111)?

According to 11:39-40, what is the relationship between the exemplars of faith from Israel's past and the author's audience?

Hebrews 12

Who makes up the "cloud [or crowd] of witnesses" in 12:1 and why are they watching the "race" run by the author's audience? How does the race analogy here compare with other appearances of the motif (1 Cor. 9:24-27; Phil. 2:16; 2 Tim. 4:7)? In what sense is the life of faith or the life of virtue more generally like or not like participation in an athletic competition?

In what sense is Jesus "the pioneer and perfecter of our faith" (12:2)?

Is "the one who is speaking" (12:25) Jesus or God? Would changing the speaker change the meaning of the text? What is the rhetorical effect of the closing description of God as "a consuming fire" (12:29)?

The author states that the assembly on the heavenly Mount Zion is a gathering of the firstborn ones (plural)? What might be the rhetorical power of this statement in the immediate context (cf. 12:16) and in the letter as a whole?

Hebrews 13

A number of scholars believe that Hebrews originally concluded with the end of Hebrews 12 and that the final chapter was added to an otherwise complete document. How might one assess this hypothesis? What evidence would support or undermine it?

Jesus Christ is "the same yesterday and today and forever" (13:8). What other texts in Hebrews does this concise statement echo or express?

From details in Hebrews 13, what can be surmised about the organizational structure or the social circumstances of the community addressed in Hebrews?

When compared with other New Testament letters, what similarities and differences can be seen in the closing chapter of Hebrews? How would various aspects of this closing relate to debates in the ancient church about Paul's authorship of the letter?

Bibliography

Aitken, Ellen Bradshaw. "Portraying the Temple in Stone and Text: The Arch of Titus and the Epistle to the Hebrews." Pages 131–48 in *Hebrews: Contemporary Methods—New Insights*. Edited by Gabriella Gelardini. Leiden: Brill, 2005.

Allen, David. "The Forgotten Spirit: A Pentecostal Reading of the Epistle to the Hebrews?" *Journal of Pentecostal Theology* 18 (2009): 51–66.

Allen, David. "The Holy Spirit as Gift or Giver? Retaining the Pentecostal Dimension of Hebrews 2.4." *The Bible Translator* 59 (2008): 151–58.

Attridge, Harold W. *The Epistle to the Hebrews*. Hermeneia. Philadelphia: Fortress, 1989.

Attridge, Harold W., and Gabriella Gelardini, eds. *Hebrews in Contexts*. Ancient Judaism and Christianity 91. Leiden: Brill, 2016.

Aune, David E. "Heracles and Christ: Heracles Imagery in the Christology of Early Christianity." Pages 3–19 in *Greeks, Romans, and Christians: Essays in Honor of Abraham J. Malherbe*. Edited by David L. Balch, Everett Ferguson, and Wayne A. Meeks. Minneapolis: Fortress, 1990.

Bates, Matthew W. *The Birth of the Trinity: Jesus, God, and Spirit in New Testament and Early Christian Interpretations of the Old Testament*. Oxford: Oxford University Press, 2015.

Bateman, Herbert W., ed. *Four Views on the Warning Passages in Hebrews*. Grand Rapids: Kregel, 2007.

Bauckham, Richard. *Jesus and the God of Israel: God Crucified and Other Studies on the New Testament's Christology of Divine Identity*. Grand Rapids: Eerdmans, 2008.

Braun, Herbert. *An die Hebräer*. Handbuch zum Neuen Testament 14. Tübingen: Mohr Siebeck, 1984.

Brown, Joanne Carlson, and Carole R. Bohn, eds. *Christianity, Patriarchy, and Abuse: A Feminist Critique*. New York: Pilgrim Press, 1989.

Bruce, Frederick Fyvie. *The Epistle to the Hebrews*. Rev. ed. New International Commentary on the New Testament. Grand Rapids: Eerdmans, 1990.

Bulley, Allen D. "Death and Rhetoric in the Hebrews 'Hymn to Faith.'" *Studies in Religion* 25 (1996): 409–23.

Bultmann, Rudolf. "New Testament and Mythology." Pages 1–44 in *Kerygma and Myth*. Edited by H. W. Bartsch. New York: Harper & Row, 1961.

Capps, Donald. *The Child's Song: The Religious Abuse of Children*. Louisville: Westminster John Knox, 1995.

Cockerill, Gareth Lee. *The Epistle to the Hebrews*. New International Commentary on the New Testament. Grand Rapids: Eerdmans, 2012.

Cosby, Michael R. *The Rhetorical Composition and Function of Hebrews 11 in the Light of Example Lists in Antiquity*. Macon: Macon University Press, 1988.

Croy, N. Clayton. *Endurance in Suffering: Hebrews 12:1-13 in its Rhetorical, Religious, and Philosophical Context*. Society for New Testament Studies Monograph Series 98. Cambridge: Cambridge University Press, 1998.

Denzinger, Heinrich, and Adolf Schönmetzer. *Enchiridion Symbolorum, Definitionum et Declarationum de Rebus Fidei et Morum*. 32nd ed. Friburg: Herder, 1963.

DeSilva, David A. *Perseverance in Gratitude: A Socio-Rhetorical Commentary on the Epistle to the Hebrews*. Grand Rapids: Eerdmans, 2000.

Docherty, Susan E. *The Use of the Old Testament in Hebrews: A Case Study in Early Jewish Bible Interpretation*. Wissenschaftliche Untersuchungen zum Neuen Testament 2.260. Tübingen: Mohr Siebeck, 2009.

Easter, Matthew C. "Faith in the God Who Resurrects: Theocentric Faith of Hebrews." *New Testament Studies* 63 (2017): 76–91.

Eisenbaum, Pamela. *The Jewish Heroes of Christian History: Hebrews 11 in Literary Context*. Society of Biblical Literature Dissertation Series 156. Atlanta: Scholars Press, 1997.

Emmrich, Martin. "'Amtscharisma': Through the Eternal Spirit (Hebrews 9:14)." *Bulletin for Biblical Research* 12 (2002a): 17–32.

Emmrich, Martin. "Pneuma in Hebrews: Prophet and Interpreter." *Westminster Theological Journal* 64 (2002b): 55–71.

Emmrich, Martin. "Hebrews 6:4-6—Again! (A Pneumatological Inquiry)." *Westminster Theological Journal* 65 (2003a): 83–96.

Emmrich, Martin. *Pneumatological Concepts in the Epistle to the Hebrews: Amtscharisma, Prophet, and Guide of the Eschatological Exodus*. Lanham, MD: University Press of America, 2003b.

Flusser, David. "'Today If You Will Listen to His Voice': Creative Jewish Exegesis in Hebrews 3–4." Pages 55–62 in *Creative Biblical Exegesis: Christian and Jewish Hermeneutics through the Centuries*. Edited by Benjamin Uffenheimer, and Henning Graf Reventlow. JSOTSup 59. Sheffield: Sheffield Academic, 1988.

Gelardini, Gabriella. "Hebrews, An Ancient Synagogue Homily for Tisha be-Av: Its Function, its Basis, its Theological Interpretation." Pages 107–27 in *Hebrews: Contemporary Methods—New Insights*. Edited by Gabriella Gelardini. Leiden: Brill, 2005.

Greenlee, J. Harold. "Hebrews 11:11: Sarah's Faith or Abraham's?" *Notes on Translation* 4.1 (1990): 37–42.

Greer, Rowan A. *The Captain of Our Salvation: A Study in the Patristic Exegesis of Hebrews*. Beiträge Zur Geschichte der Biblischen Exegese 15. Tübingen: Mohr Siebeck, 1973.

Hahn, Scott W. "Covenant, Cult, and the Curse-of-Death: *Diathēkē* in Heb 9:15-22." Pages 65–88 in *Hebrews: Contemporary Methods—New Insights*. Edited by Gabriella Gelardini. Leiden: Brill, 2005

Hamm, Dennis. "Faith in the Epistle to the Hebrews: The Jesus Factor." *Catholic Biblical Quarterly* 52 (1990): 270–91.

Hay, David M. *Glory at the Right Hand: Psalm 110 in Early Christianity*. Society of Biblical Literature Monograph Series 18. Nashville: Abingdon, 1973.

Heen, Erik M., and Philip W. D. Krey, eds. *Hebrews*. Ancient Christian Commentary on Scripture. Downers Grove, IL: InterVarsity, 2005.

Hodson, Alan K. "Hebrews." Pages 226–37 in *A Biblical Theology of the Holy Spirit*. Edited by Trevor J. Burke and Keith Warrington. Eugene, OR: Cascade Books, 2014.

Hoppin, Ruth. *Priscilla: Author of the Epistle to the Hebrews, and Other Essays*. New York: Exposition, 1969.

Horbury, William. "The Aaronic Priesthood in the Epistle to the Hebrews." *Journal for the Study of the New Testament* 19 (1983): 43–71.

Horton, Fred. *The Melchizedek Tradition: A Critical Examination of the Sources to the Fifth Century A.D. and in the Epistle to the Hebrews*. Society for New Testament Studies Monograph Series 30. Cambridge: Cambridge University Press, 1976.

Hurst, Lincoln Douglas. *The Epistle to the Hebrews: Its Background of Thought*. Society for New Testament Studies Monograph Series 65. Cambridge: Cambridge University Press, 1990.

Johnson, Luke Timothy. *Hebrews: A Commentary*. New Testament Library. Louisville: Westminster John Knox, 2006.

Kitchen, Robert A. "Making the Imperfect Perfect: The Adaptation of Hebrews 11 in the 9th Mēmrā of the Syriac Book of Steps." Pages 227–52 in *The Reception and Interpretation of the Bible in Late Antiquity*. Edited by Lorenzo DiTommaso and Lucian Turcescu. Leiden: Brill, 2008.

Kittredge, Cynthia Briggs. "Hebrews." Pages 428–52 in *Searching the Scriptures, Vol. 2: A Feminist Commentary*. Edited by Elisabeth Schüssler Fiorenza. New York: Crossroad, 1994.

Klauck, Hans-Josef. "Sacrifice and Sacrificial Offerings (NT)." *Anchor Bible Dictionary* 5 (1992): 890.

Koester, Craig R. *Hebrews*. Anchor Bible 36. New York: Doubleday, 2001.

Koester, Craig R. "Hebrews, Rhetoric, and the Future of Humanity." *Catholic Biblical Quarterly* 64 (2002): 103–23.

Laansma, Jon C., and Daniel J Treier, eds. *Christology, Hermeneutics, and Hebrews: Profiles from the History of Interpretation*. Library of New Testament Studies 423. London: T&T Clark, 2012.

Lane, William L. *Hebrews*. 2 Vols. Word Biblical Commentary 47A-B. Dallas: Word Books, 1991.

Lee, Gregory W. *Today When You Hear His Voice: Scripture, the Covenants, and the People of God*. Grand Rapids: Eerdmans, 2016.

Lee, John A. L. "Hebrews 5:14 and *Hexis*: A History of Misunderstanding." *Novum Testamentum* 39 (1997): 151–76.

Lehne, Susanne. *The New Covenant in Hebrews*. Journal for the Study of the New Testament: Supplement Series 44. Sheffield: JSOT Press, 1990.

Levison, Jack. "A Theology of the Spirit in the Letter to the Hebrews." *Catholic Biblical Quarterly* 78 (2016): 90–110.

Lindars, Barnabas. *The Theology of the Letter to the Hebrews*. New Testament Theology. Cambridge: Cambridge University Press, 1991.

Long, Stephen D. *Hebrews*. Belief: A Theological Commentary on the Bible. Louisville: Westminster John Knox, 2011.

Mackie, Scott D. "Visually Oriented Rhetoric and Visionary Experience in Hebrews 12:1-4." *Catholic Biblical Quarterly* 79 (2017): 476–97.

Mitchell, Alan C. *Hebrews*. Sacra Pagina 13. Collegeville, MN: Liturgical Press, 2007.

Moffitt, David M. *Atonement and the Logic of Resurrection in the Epistle to the Hebrews*. Supplements to Novum Testamentum 141. Leiden: Brill, 2011.

Moore, Nicholas J. *Repetition in Hebrews: Plurality and Singularity in the Letter to the Hebrews, Its Ancient Context, and the Early Church*. Wissenschaftliche Untersuchungen zum Neuen Testament 2.388. Tübingen: Mohr Siebeck, 2015.

Motyer, Stephen. "The Spirit in Hebrews: No Longer Forgotten." Pages 213–27 in *The Spirit and Christ in the New Testament and Christian Theology: Essays in Honor of Max Turner*. Edited by I. Howard Marshall, Volker Rabens, and Cornelis Bennema. Grand Rapids: Eerdmans, 2012.

Nicole, Roger. "Some Comments on Hebrews 6:4-6 and the Doctrine of the Perseverance of God with the Saints." Pages 355–64 in *Current Issues in Biblical and Patristic Interpretation: Studies in Honor of Merrill C. Tenney*. Edited by Gerald F. Hawthorne. Grand Rapids: Eerdmans, 1975.

O'Brien, Peter T. *God Has Spoken in His Son: A Biblical Theology of Hebrews*. Downers Grove, IL: InterVarsity, 2016.

Panofsky, Erwin, ed. *Abbot Suger on the Abbey Church of Saint-Denis and Its Art Treasures*. 2nd ed. Princeton: Princeton University Press, 1979.

Peterson, David. *Hebrews and Perfection: An Examination of the Concept of Perfection in the "Epistle to the Hebrews"*. Society for New Testament Studies Monograph Series 47. Cambridge: Cambridge University Press, 1982.

Pierce, Madison N. "Hebrews 3.7–4.11 and the Spirit's Speech to the Community." Pages 173–84 in *Muted Voices of the New Testament: Readings in the Catholic Epistles and Hebrews*. Edited by Katherine M. Hockey,

Madison N. Pierce, and Francis Watson. Library of New Testament Studies 565. London: T&T Clark, 2017.

Rittgers, Ronald K., ed. *Hebrews, James*. Reformation Commentary on Scripture. Downers Grove, IL: InterVarsity, 2017.

Rothschild, Clare K. *Hebrews As Pseudepigraphon: The History and Significance of the Pauline Attribution of Hebrews*. Wissenschaftliche Untersuchungen zum Neuen Testament 1.235. Tübingen: Mohr Siebeck, 2009.

Schenck, Kenneth J. "A Celebration of the Enthroned Son: The Catena of Hebrews 1." *Journal of Biblical Literature* 120 (2001): 469–85.

Steyn, Gert. *A Quest for the Assumed LXX Vorlage of the Explicit Quotations in Hebrews*. Forschungen zur Religion und Literatur des Alten und NeuenTestaments 235. Göttingen: Vandenhoeck & Ruprecht, 2011.

Stranahan, Brainerd P. "Bunyan and the Epistle to the Hebrews: His Source for the Idea of Pilgrimage in 'The Pilgrim's Progress.'" *Studies in Philology* 79 (1982): 279–96.

Svartvik, Jesper. "Reading the Epistle to the Hebrews without Presupposing Supersessionism." Pages 77–91 in *Christ Jesus and the Jewish People Today: New Explorations of Theological Interrelationships*. Edited by Philip A. Cunningham. Grand Rapids: Eerdmans, 2011.

Svartvik, Jesper. "Stumbling Block or Stepping Stone? On the Reception History of Hebrews 8:13." Pages 316–42 in *Hebrews in Contexts*. Edited by Harold W. Attridge, and Gabriella Gelardini. Ancient Judaism and Early Christianity 91. Leiden: Brill, 2016.

Swete, Henry B. *The Holy Spirit in the New Testament*. London: Macmillan, 1910.

Swetnam, James. "The Crux at Hebrews 5,7–8." *Biblica* 81 (2000): 347–61.

Swetnam, James. *Jesus and Isaac: A Study of the Epistle to the Hebrews in the Light of the Aqedah*. Rome: Biblical Institute Press, 1981.

Tabbernee, William. "To Pardon or Not to Pardon." Pages 375–86 in *Critica et Philologica, Nachleben, First Two Centuries, Tertullian to Arnobius, Egypt before Nicaea, Athanasius and his Opponents*. Edited by Maurice F. Wiles, and Edward J. Yarnold. Studia Patristica 36. Leuven: Peeters, 2001.

Thiessen, Matthew. "Hebrews and the End of the Exodus." *Novum Testamentum* 49 (2007): 353–69.

Thiselton, Anthony C. *The Holy Spirit —In Biblical Teaching, through the Centuries, and Today*. Grand Rapids: Eerdmans, 2013.

Thompson, James. *The Beginnings of Christian Philosophy: The Epistle to the Hebrews*. Catholic Biblical Quarterly Monograph Series 13. Washington, DC: Catholic Biblical Association of America, 1982.

Torgerson, Mark A. "Hebrews in the Worship Life of the Church: A Historical Survey." Pages 269–96 in *Reading the Epistle to the Hebrews*. Edited by Eric F. Mason and Kevin B. McCruden. Resources for Biblical Study 66. Atlanta: SBL, 2011.

Vanhoye, Albert. *The Letter to the Hebrews: A New Commentary*. Trans. L. Arnold. New York; Mahwah, NJ: Paulist, 2015.

Vanhoye, Albert. *Structure and Message of the Epistle to the Hebrews*. Subsidia Biblica 12. Rome: Pontifical Biblical Institute, 1989.

Williamson, Ronald. "Platonism and Hebrews." *Scottish Journal of Theology* 16 (1963): 415–24.

Wills, Lawrence. "The Form of the Sermon in Hellenistic Judaism and Early Christianity." *Harvard Theological Review* 77 (1984): 277–99.

Young, Frances "Christological Ideas in the Greek Commentaries on the Epistle to the Hebrews." *Journal of Theological Studies* 20 (1969): 150–63.

Index